NOTES FROM THE PLAYGROUND

These stories are for my mother, Colette.
She was my first and most faithful reader.

notes from the playground

GREG JOHN

I am grateful beyond words to Kevin, Christopher, Collin, Marian, Meredith, Megan, Jon, Kate, and Adrienne who held me up when I just about quit this project. I could not and would not have completed this 'megillah' without you! These tales tell my story now.

May they bring clarity and comfort, wherever they may roam.

Order of Events

Foreword

By Jill Vialet, Founder and CEO of Playworks

I first met Greg John out on the playground at the school where he served as principal. From that moment I knew that he understood the power of play to bring out the best in every kid. It also became quickly clear that Greg was one of the most curious people I'd ever met, and that despite the very real demands of being a principal, he had figured out a way to approach the job with an openness and excitement that was really uncommon. When I learned that he was sharing his observations in writing, I was thrilled.

Over the years, Greg and I have shared concerns about the priorities in public education, including how schools often treat recess as a necessary evil: alternating between paying it little attention or taking it away to punish bad behavior. Compounding this circumstance is the fact that it's all too easy to dismiss play as frivolous, a distraction from the "real" work of learning.

What both of us recognized is that recess is both an opportunity and challenge hiding in plain sight. Left unattended, it represents a real danger to school climate and contributes to the larger and unhealthy trend of glorifying "busy." But with a little attention, recess represents an incredible opportunity to build community, and create experiential learning opportunities that promote essential social and emotional skills. Greg John is someone who has built community and who recognizes the importance of empathy, teamwork, leadership and inclusion in helping students succeed.

Play theorist Brian Sutton-Smith wrote, "The opposite of play is not work, the opposite of play is depression." In Greg's writing, he underscores how play contributes to kids' physical and emotional well-being, their academic achievement and their capacity for trust, self-control and conflict resolution. Through play, children complete their journeys. Far from frivolous, play is high stakes developmental work, making a greater contribution to how a child sees himself than many of the things children are asked to do in schools.

I find in Greg's work a much-needed and empathic focus on the child's perspective, where the playground is recognized as the place where it all happens. Play is kids' work. It's experiential learning that contributes directly to a person's ability to handle failure, to work in teams, and to take risks.

In Greg's vignettes, I get carried back to what happens to a child's spirit when he or she steps onto this asphalt proving ground. The impact of experiences there spill over into classrooms, homes, jobs, and relationships. Events there will shape the causes and conditions that determine the direction of children's lives.

Ultimately, play matters because people matter and it represents a tremendous opportunity for people to get to know one another — to see and be seen by others. Play is a powerful tool, capable of fostering the qualities within children that will lead them toward becoming the people we so desperately need.

Greg's stories chart the unfolding of young hearts as children stand up, get knocked down, and stand once again. We are engaged, directly engaged, in the work needed to build healthy communities. For me, **Notes from the Playground** reminds adults of the world that a child sees, and in sharing that perspective, offers the chance for us to get outside ourselves and imagine a world our kids deserve — one which will enable them to grow up and become the grown-ups we so desperately need them to become.

Starting Point

When I first visited the school on the hill, summer heat baked the dead grass covering much of the open space there. A windowed and white concrete block — the school building — shoved itself into the hillside as a misfit among the rocks, broken glass, discarded sofas, and random car parts.

In my work shoes and blue jeans, I crunched my way across a goat trail that wound through the weeds and debris. I found the hill's highest point, became still, and then got touched by a spirit that must have lived in this place. Current shot up through my feet so that even in the heat, I felt a chill.

Oh my God!

I mouthed these words through dry lips as I looked toward the bay, the old shipyards, the freeway, and the crumbling parts of the city. I knew folks in the neighborhoods there who told tales of hard times and mean streets. In the opposite direction, if I leaned just so, I could see across the flats toward the distant bridge and the gateway to the ocean. Storms, fog, wind, and the setting sun came from that side.

The school here was to be my school.

My family and I came back a week later with a huge bag of poppy seeds. We had this idea to seed the entire hill so that it would explode in orange come springtime. We all took big hands full and cast seeds everywhere. I predicted that when the flowers bloomed, so would the school. I remember seeing three boys that day, ebony skinned, hair breeze-bobbing, wirey and naked to the waist. They were maybe seven or eight years old, free to run among the stalks of dried grass, no grown up in sight. In spite of terrain pocked with glass and metal shards, none of these boys wore shoes.

They looked at me looking at them and then they dashed out of site. See you soon. . .

As it turned out, I got my prophecy backward. Months later, after rains, some poppies did bloom, but I knew by then that I had just started to understand how I stood when I stood on that hill. To call it magical came close. Stories surfaced each day, bits and pieces that wiggled up from the gravel, the school walls or the playground grit. I learned that first, before the talking, I had to listen. What came before my time to bring this school to this place? How did I fit in?

The playground made only one command: Write down and do not edit what I tell you. The rest will take care of itself. And my life as a school principal took a new direction born of this place — one that could not have come from anywhere else. Love, hate, spite, joy, sugar and salt. All of it mixing. All of it coming on in a tumult each day.

Poppies grow all over the hillside now. This kind of change takes years and not months. I find I have been turned inside out and then outside in again. The playground helped me lose my old self. I found a new self ready to step up. That's how it goes up here. Like an ancient rhythm, that's the way it was meant to be.

Rules

Admit that you are a child wrapped in a grown up body.

Go backward in time to go forward in life.

Treasure the bites and the stings of your first mistakes.

Re-think, re-do, and re-write your soul's story.

Make for yourself a life that you can no longer predict.

Fall down, get up, and go again.

Dance in the rain, sing all day, talk to animals and see forever.

Locate, in yourself, the strength to stand tall and to bend.

1.

September
First Days

"First in line?"

"Yep!"

"How come you have to be first all the time?"

"What do you mean?"

"Look behind you."

"And?"

"Twenty other places to be, but you have to be up front."

"First is where I want to be."

"Do you ever wonder why?"

"That's just the way I am."

Seed

If you want to know what 'brave' looks like in a child, you have to let go of what you think you know. Shrink yourself down to no more than a few feet tall. Take away the cool confidence that comes from experience — the times you stood up, got knocked down, and then stood up again. Take away everything, even the word 'brave' itself. At three-foot two, brave may not yet be in your vocabulary.

Two words you might try — 'by myself' — as when Jamie, for example, a four and a half year old, learned the meaning of these two words. She had to take them head on just this week when, on Monday before school, her mother left her on the sidewalk of screaming and grimy streets that intersect about ten blocks from the school.

She left her there (she later told me) because she forgot to count the kids as they piled into her car. She further forgot to count as they hopped out in front of the school. She still hadn't counted when I met them all in front of the school and asked — Where's Jamie? She stopped, looked and then we counted together.

Panic came next. She made a tight yelp, now leaving the other four children with me. She jumped in her smoking beater of a wagon and sped away. I had images of Jamie, cut off from the rest, a tiny being. I have no reliable account for what the mother did next. I know only what I saw and felt.

For example, I felt my pulse race as I paced the sidewalk. The heart rate did not slow as I looked down the street where I had last seen the smoking car. To the west, no sign of anyone coming. Then, to the east, past an oak tree and a stop sign, I saw a little girl, Jamie, making her way up the hill, over-sized backpack about as large as she. She had her hands shoved in her pockets, and a little dark cloud hovered over her head. She stopped, looked up, and then entered the school building.

Bravery comes when it has to — when you come face-to-face with something bigger than you. It comes when you sort out the gap between faith and fact, when you look over your shoulder and discover you have only yourself to count on. It comes because the option for its opposite has disappeared. You give up a great deal to acquire bravery — like the dreamy trust in those whom you thought you could count on. Bravery makes a mark that assures a little girl like Jamie will not forget this day.

The beater came back-firing and barreling up the hill. I met her at the car door and told her that her daughter had gone to class. Take a few minutes before you go in, I told her. You can make things right later. Not now.

A story would grow over this day the way a scab grows over a wound. Jamie would carry forward whatever she needed to — the memory of before and after and the knowledge that she figured out the way all on her own. First steps happen when we learn to lift our chins and take our licks. The greatest gift comes when we learn to do this without closing our hearts.

All in good time, my little angel. All in good time.

3

Wham

Wham! A shoe thuds against the front door to the school. Bam! Door flies open and collides with smudged wall tile. Pow! Framed in the doorway, punched out in back-lit sunrise silhouette stands Jeremiah. He whips his book bag from his shoulder and slams it on the floor. Then, he pulls up his hood, shoves his hands in his jeans pockets, and floor-kicks his way to the closest corner. Tears stream and this boy is angry!

Other adults scurry away. He and I remain, the only two in the hallway. I won't walk away. This one is mine. So, I ask myself how to help him move through this place and onto the next. No good to stay here. I decide to launch another one of my on-the-spot rituals, woven with a bit of science and some other things I'll just make up. Jeremiah, I say, do you know about the triple-water cure? At least he looks up, wet-faced and puffing.

I tell him that whenever you get a powerful emotion like anger in your body, you have to move it through. If it gets stuck, it can make you sick. So, I take him to the water cooler in the office, fill three Dixie cup of cold water, and tell him he will have to gulp one right after the other. That will wash it through and you'll feel better. But it won't be easy. Three cups is a lot of water! He nods just once, but enough to allow me to go on.

Sudden opportunities like the one with Jeremiah wake me up. I remember them later when they pop back into mind, shining like little pearls. I sit with these stories and let them show me how much happens around me, all the time. I know, for example, that of the hundreds of people show up at the doors to my school, some walk, ride, stumble, and some collapse through the door. Mine is to practice bending, opening, and receiving the shapes that come with grace and gratitude.

For example, one of the adults who scurried out when Jeremiah came in was a parent, often critical of certain 'elements' that attend our school. When the boy burst in, she paused, looked down, pulled her purse in close, and slipped out. Her economy of motion brought to mind how the ability to make way for another is rare. Where the intent to serve aligns with the will to learn, change becomes probable. Where one person turns another into an 'element' opportunities diminish. Still, I need to seek a way to welcome even her.

My impromptu spell works. Jeremiah lines up the three Dixie cups on top of the water cooler — like the 'kid' from an old Western, staggering in off the high desert and stepping up to the bar for a triple medicinal. He knocks back one, two, and pauses midway through the third. We wait together. Then, down the hatch, a smile, and out the door. In this way, we get through the first half hour.

I want a flexible mind that makes way for the wish each body has to find balance, make things right, and find connection. That skill waits for the invitation and comes when I make more room for myself. What better way than this to grow into days that are a bit bigger than what we might have expected?

Reverie

I see Jacinda alone in one of the school's breezeways. She dances a kind of three-hop number, a light skip down the middle, then back the way she came. She sings to herself as well — a quiet, private song. As I come around the corner, I can hear just a few notes.

Concrete above and to the sides frames her in a rectangle of light. Behind her, I see the expanse of empty playground. A bit farther, a chain link fence. Beyond the fence, four lanes of traffic. September rain has fallen and the asphalt grit glistens.

I remain at the breezeway's far end, about thirty yards away. Cold air lingers the way cold often does in the between spaces among concrete buildings. As soon as I see her, I know she is in a place of her own — one that I cannot access except to witness. She dances as she pleases, and the word that comes to me is delight.

How true that reverie comes less often to me now! I may have to bring it on more by force than by accident. As a boy, the glow of daydreams came to me all the time. Now, I fill the emptiness with a next step or a change of subject. Jacinda, however, demonstrates no hesitation in acquiring reverie. She slips into dancing with invisible friends and wanders her realm with a sure foot. At one with her steps, with the sweet breeze, with her humming, she pirouettes just outside of the roar and the rush of circumstance.

I call her name and she comes to a full stop. I know that I have interrupted. I question myself. Why did I do that? I fall into a brief moment of self-reflection against the mirror of her non-time and non-place. I see that I am curious about how a child travels to a place I once knew, but no longer know how to find.

She looks at me. She waits. Her eyes ask "Yes?" as in "how may I help you?" I come to understand that I am uninvited, but not in a mean way. I step forward from the breezeway shadows, almost tiptoeing, and move on. I hear the hum and know she has started dancing again. I look back and wave as I turn away.

Enchantment remains for me, but more as a faint glimmer, connected, but far away. Soft exchanges of light and dark, instances that slip below and rise again. My own dance with memory and time can come to me that way. The quieter spirits get dismissed, replaced by rougher, cruder shapes.

To step in between as if no distinction between in and out existed — that's what a child can teach us! Ears tuned to the quarter tones and eyes to the shimmers just beyond the prism. Whether I hold or dismiss them with a harrumph has no bearing. At midlife, I feel time's quickening. But I also get a lift from knowing that a child, by dancing, offers a kind of proof for that which I can no longer see.

Trouble

Red and gold leaves wafted down onto the empty playground this morning and blustery winds pushed the leaves along. I breathed in through my nose. Above, storm clouds blanketed the hillside in gray.

Ah, sweet wet air!

As I stood, I drifted among pre-storm ions and boyhood memories of long ago. Running in rain, sucking in cold air, getting wet, loving all of it.

Now, wind came on a second time, dropping more leaves. Through this tumbling curtain of fall color, my dreaming paused as a boy stepped onto the playground, following three paces behind mother. The pair walked a few feet from me, speechless. He gave me a glance and I could see that he, Espy, brought his own kind of weather.

The curly haired, scrappy boy shuffled along in green shoes and jeans so big that they drooped below his back side. This outfit was his norm, so I saw nothing out of whack. Even the red bandana, tied off with one end skyward and the other to the side, fell within his usual range.

What I did not see? This boy, running, screaming, climbing, hanging upside down, and scratching his belly. Today, he was not himself. Instead, he traipsed behind mother as she slinked in her tight maroon and black dress, four-inch heels, and alligator handbag.

The pair crossed the four-square courts, boy scratching behind ear, and mother, chin up ignoring him. Once at the bench, she yanked his belt loop to make him sit next to her.

They both sat up, however, when Nelson, Espy's best friend, scrambled over the east fence and ran toward the play structure. These boys were almost twins except that one wore a bandana and the other a backward green cap. Seeing Nelson, Espy lit up. Hey Nelson! — but mother tugged him back down.

Not so fast, son.

So, with boy's face cloudier still, he remained seated. Nelson, meanwhile, kept climbing. When he reached the apex of the play structure, he turned toward his friend as if to ask — Espy, can you play with me?

Not today, friend. This bird was grounded.

I had no intention of interfering with mother and son. However, their interaction brought flashbacks of my boyhood — about being in trouble all the time. Once I heard my second grade teacher talking to the principal: "What's the point in boys? They are nothing more than mistakes in motion. Complete nuisances." Indeed, the other nun nodded.

My dreams snapped again as the rain came on. Time to get indoors. I blew my whistle. Children spilled in from far courts. Espy's mother, meanwhile, let her son get up. As he ran by me, he smacked my hand in a low five. Then, his mother approached.

"Please don't encourage him," she said and then, as she turned — "What I'd do for a girl!"

What? Oh no! Come back, I said. But she declined so I let her go. What a shame! She was missing out. For inside, she could have seen explorers, dreamers, cloud kissers, fighters and peacemakers of the future all jockeying for their place under clear or cloudy skies. Not one mistake here. Instead, apprentices awakening, sparring, and searching for at least one fair witness to this short storm called boyhood.

6

Papa

You have to walk down two flights of stairs to get to the playground. This path leads out through battered metal doors propped open by two ancient trashcans — one can on each side. Monday morning, Felicia hid just outside and to the right. When I reached the doorway, she popped out in front of me and yelled "Papa!"

My coffee flew and she took off squealing toward the far side of the yard. Even at six and a half, this scrawny scruff of a neighborhood kid knew how to make a grown man jump.

She had been calling me Papa, staring at me, looking about a half inch from crazy for about a week. None of it sat well. For neighborhood kids, mothers often run the show. Many of my students have to work hard to fill in the blanks where a father is supposed to go. No trifling matter.

So, I was perplexed. I knew little about Felicia. She had been a first grader here for two months, entered the school after weeks where she had not been in any school at all. She had one cousin in second grade. Besides scaring me, she spent time looking out for her cousin mostly to know where the older girl was. And while I knew little about Felicia, I knew less about her mother except to see her dropping her daughter off each day, sporting some big tattoos.

But the young girl's antics had reached the point of distraction. Late yesterday, I dug up all I could learn about her. I found more missing pieces. No father (not on the card), no brothers or sisters, and then these patches of time where she'd fall out of one school and show up at another. Quite a bumpy ride, at least on paper.

Therefore, yesterday morning, I went out the front door of the school, through the alley along the north side of the playground, and up the east steps of the yard. I got to the point where I could see the big double doors and sure enough, there she crouched, waiting for me. I always wear these super cushy shoes — my interceptors — because they allow me to walk up behind pranksters and catch them seconds prior a bad choice. I approached in silence and came up behind Felicia. Too easy!

"Looking for someone?" I said from about a foot away. This time, she did the jumping, but when she looked up, I saw fear that comes on a face when a child thinks she's going to get hit. I told her "Calm. Calm. Don't be scared. I just want to talk."

She relaxed a bit: "You been calling me papa for a bunch of days and today we are going to turn the page." She blinked, but seemed unable to speak. "Time for me to get to know you and for you to get to know me for real. No more papa. No more games."

As I jot my thoughts down this afternoon, I am noting that she didn't call out to me all day. In fact, she didn't talk to anyone. Yesterday's intervention might have caused a full stop but I know better than to leave it like that. Time to open a second door since the former one slammed shut. No more games. Instead, an invitation for her to come out and begin filling in some missing pieces.

My heart is in it if she can find hers. We will have to see how things unfold.

Hood

I waited by the back gate to the playground this morning, watching as a pack of twenty three damp eight-year-olds came up the hill. Tossed out from a broken-axeled bus more than a block away and now plagued by drizzle and wet wind. They shuffled up the back steps, hoods pulled. No one looked up. Thick fog penetrated everything. Even the inside of my jacket pockets got wet.

Even though the clock said 'recess', no one was waiting outside. All of us were waiting just inside the doors in a huge entry hall. Still, we were too many for the space. And the cold came in with the kids. I saw child after child hunching down, looking for a way to get warm. Wet shoes, drooping back packs, soaked and drooping hoods. I heard one fifth grader calling out, "Who turned off the heat?"

But the morning had something heavier than the cold air. No one said hello, either. Not a single good morning, hi there, hey, howdy, or any of hello's twelve thousand other cousins. For eight year-olds, I might understand, but the wet blanket fell everywhere.

I said to myself — start moving. My mother advised me as a boy to move when you felt the coldness or even a sadness coming on. If you can move, you can hope, she once said. And, I started nudging the kids to do the same. I walked along the hall where all of us waited for the opening bell, checking in like a medic from hunched hoodie to the next. Rules didn't allow the kids upstairs before 8:40, so it seemed we were all stuck.

Then, I looked out a small, slot window of the back door and noticed that not all of us had come inside. A nine year old named Sylvia stood at the center of the kick-ball court, no hood, and not even a jacket on. There, against the gray sky and the thick fog, she smiled and bounced a ball with a face that had an invitation written across it: Do you want to play? A huge set of white teeth as she smiled.

"Hey y'all. Let's go outside. There's more room outside than in!"

Kids looked at me, then at each other, and then toward the door. Sylvia kept looking in from the outside, radiating sunshine and warmth that lit things up no matter what the sky might be saying.

"Let's go, boys and girls. We can do this!"

Moans rose up, but children filed out. Recess, as an act of defiance, would soon begin. Sylvia called a group of friends over and a kick ball game rolled into motion.

The morning — even the entire start of the day — came down to one child. What would happen had we come to school but found no one and nothing other than wet, dark, and down? What would we do? Where would we go from there?

We did not have that today. We had the gift of the exceptions. Proof that you can re-write the ending to any story, and evidence that the day you have is the day you make. How lucky we were to have a child in our midst to remind us of this super power.

Ziggy

Monday came on in a quiet soft way. I waited at the gate on the far side of the playground where I stand most days to greet the kids as they come. No one, however, had come just yet and I as I looked down the hill, I could see nothing stirring. Then, from the streets just down the hill, I heard a familiar whistle. A sweet little melody that bounced off the walls of the housing units. I knew who the melody came from, too.

In a minute, I saw Ziggy, a skinny little boy, whom I could spot on and off as he bolted through the alleys. His joints, his jeans, and his over-long fabric belt hung on him like someone else's clothes. He wore a borrowed and shredded shirt — no coat or gloves even on cold days. His hair capped it off — an explosion of black and brown and blond that wafted and bobbed with each skip.

Buoyed along by his self-made melody — I saw a boy who could turn a quiet start like today's into a sunrise grin.

I didn't know a lot about him. He had been on my roster. He didn't come to my school anymore. Then on the first day of school, he whistled to the gate, turned left, and kept on whistling. He didn't arrive to class that day or the next.

I requested an investigation, but facts were few. I found out only that his mom drove a truck. She was on the road most days leaving Ziggy with aunties, uncles, friends of friends. People fed him, gave him a floor or a sofa.

On this Monday, I could follow his path by listening to the looping notes he weaved. I could see him going door to door, stepping inside one apartment, then popping out the back door of another. A moment later, he showed up at the corner store, hanging? and bumming a hit on what these young men smoked or taking a swig from their brown-wrapped bottles.

I want my school to have a place for every child. But every child can't fit inside this school's fences. When a one-of-a-kind comes, he can get tagged with a name: a homeless kid, latch-key, truant, a sad story. But I want the upside to show through. How would I talk of the great big world if I looked out from within Ziggy's heart and mind?

One of the neighborhood aunties expressed a wish that this child would find himself, that his mother might park her truck and get her life grounded — that they would both find a right way for themselves. She wished without hope that the boy's life might be other than a short one. Ziggy met these wishes with whistling. I got a persistent mystery that evaded disclosure in the way a pocket of air can hide inside a pair of cupped hands.

Time to turn away from my vigil. Kids began to fill the yard and I snapped back from reverie of roads, wrecks and wandering. Ziggy would be that boy able to travel in places I have never been. What if? What might? Who might? All moot. Here I am, standing, taking care of those who come, able to ask where they might go.

A look at my watch showed just seconds until the bell. Once again, it would be time to line it up.

Moods can spread. They transmit like energy and grow like fire. Whatever that energy passes through gets changed. When groups of children get together, they are themselves, but they are also another being born of their combined energy.

Sunrise

The night before last, I could not sleep. Nothing new with that. I gave up, got up, and decided to go to school early. Instead of going into my office, I walked in the front door, out the back, and across the blacktop to the place I call my spot.

I go to this place on the far side of my school's playground to collect my thoughts and relocate the horizon on confusing days. This particular spot is a sweet one. It looks out over parts of the Hill, and then, onto the Bay itself. I can see the cranes in the old shipyard, bent like ancient guardians, waiting for ships that won't come in.

From the hilltop today, I could see the earliest glow of an orange sunrise warm the sky, lighting up a few wispy clouds overhead. The geometry of the streets below remained hidden in darkness. I leaned against the damp chain link fence, completing the loops of thought that kept me awake.

However, I got a small surprise on this day. It began with warmth that found a way into my bones. Then it warmed further until I wondered whether I might be glowing from the top of my head. Well, this is different, I thought.

Then the worry left my body. The reaching left my arms. I had a moment where I lacked for nothing. Right here is enough! I said out loud.

How different from other times where I drove myself to tears by asking, hoping, wishing for some kind of rescue for myself and for these kids. In the glow of the sunrise, I saw myself as a small spark of consciousness. Though smaller than small, I am still part of everything. I am and I belong.

All of this came through before 6:15am!

A parent had written me the day before, telling me that the school needed to decide who it served. He had said that the kids on the hill were holding us back. Let them go to school in a place that's right for them, he had written. He asked for his child to be parted from the common herd. Divide this gifted child, from the slow ones. I could not imagine the kind of world that he asked for.

Sunrise allowed the toxin of those words to leave me. One tribe. All in. No escape. Just so. As the sky brightened, I felt room in me for appreciation. What I achieved arose through the way I was connected. I didn't need to cling to any of it.

Then, I lifted my head and got a second surprise. It was bright enough now that I could see the hillside below. I could make out a woman looking toward the sunrise from her back porch. I saw another man, standing on his roof, looking skyward. And, I noticed a boy standing no more that twenty feet from me next to the bent tetherball pole- one of our fifth graders, Kamani, warming to the sunrise just as I was. The sun lifted off the horizon and the day was on.

I slipped back into the building, dashed up the stairs, turned on the lights in the office and opened the window. No matter what I hoped for, what would be would be — experience that we would make together. In the early glow I knew that I had sufficient light to carry on.

Water

A third grader, Monica, tugged on my coat the other day because she wanted to tell me about an assignment her teacher had given; to write messages and place them in bottles. The teacher had promised that they would have a chance to walk down the hill to the Bay and float their messages out. They would then have a chance to write what-if stories about the journeys their little bits of paper might go on.

"Mine might make it to the other side of the planet!" She went on to share how she had crafted the message, how she planned to place the cork so that it would not leak, and how she would know for sure that her message had arrived.

"I will put a stamp in my bottle so that the person can mail me a letter!"

At lunchtime, I stood on the playground and looked at the bay. Monica's story brought up some emotions that I hadn't expected. I looked through the fence toward the bay and pictured myself as a castaway stuck on a lonely island, doing what she would do by stuffing a note into a bottle and floating it out into the waves. I pictured my message drifting, defying odds and ducking storms so that it would reach a helpful person.

Why these thoughts? Did I need a bit of a rescue?

More, what ate at me was the circular nature of challenges I managed. I had the sense that, in spite of my efforts, nothing changed. Was I at a point where I would just have to accept things as is?

"No." I whispered out loud. "That's not the way I am made."

How best to use my time on this island-of-mind? To imagine possibilities. Otherwise, my time would be nothing more than waiting for elements to take their toll.

Kids bring gifts just by being themselves. Monica gave me the start that I needed when she tugged on my coat. Anyone — a child or a bruised grown up can find a new way across the ocean. However improbable, one has to hold on. Quitting is not an option. Just as when I feel myself sinking below the surface, my soul knows to paddle upward. Upward. My body, if not my brain, reminds me what to do.

If you would have asked me at sunrise, I wouldn't have had much to offer. Now, at mid day, I can see the pragmatic necessity of hope. It's not an illusion. It's linked to survival — the soul's urge to swim, breach the surface of the water and find air. That's how we make things change and how we get around the urge to quit.

Some messages, scratched on weathered paper, float across wild and tumbling seas. They may get slammed below by storm driven waves. They may bob in the doldrums for weeks. And, it's also true that some find their way past all forms of weather to the right person in the right place at the right time. If it can happen in a little girl's dreams, it can happen for real in a grown man's life.

Asking

When I got the nine o'clock call from Ms. James' in Room 209, I knew why she called. "Would you come upstairs and take Francena for a bit? She's having one of those days. I can't get my class started."

"One of those days" meant that Francena had come to school full of questions. On such days, she would ask about everything. She would begin during the line-up on the playground, continue on the stairs up to the second floor, and then crescendo as the rest of the students dropped off their backpacks and gathered in morning circle on the rug. Hundreds of questions like:

Why do finger nails grow? Or what happens if I hold my breath forever? or Why do grown ups' feet smell? Or Ms. James, how come you always look mad? She did not mean disrespect as far as her teacher (and I) could see. She simply could not rest until she had an answer.

I arrived at the door to the classroom. Ms. James and Francena were waiting there for me. She placed the second grader's hand in mine, and said thank you. I looked at the little girl. "Want to go for a walk?"

The eyes said yes so down the hall we went.

She had a little, cobbled together frame, big eyes, bangs that she cut herself, a large mouth with full lips — well suited to asking question after question. She also liked to stick her tongue out when she smiled.

As we walked down the front steps, she asked why I wore black socks. "How come you didn't wear green? Green is a better color." Good point, Francena. Outside on the playground, we worked our way around the perimeter — our standard route on these questioning days.

The girl investigated everything. She lifted lids on trash cans, looked underneath benches, and peered through windows into classrooms. She also could hop from a standing position to a table top and she demonstrated this skill to me as our walk progressed.

I plodded along, one foot in front of the other answering her questions in single words or I-don't-knows. And, I followed as she bounced from table to bench and down again. I had hoped that one or two turns around the yard would calm her, but so far, no go.

Then, she stopped, turned, and looked at me. "Principal, how come you got old?"

This particular question got me. It was a real one and needed a real answer this time. So, I stopped, took a breath, felt my two feet beneath me and said:

"People like me have to get old. That's how we make room for you to be young. That's the way it works, Francena. You can't have one without the other."

We resumed our walk, now in silence. I brought her up the back stairs to her classroom. She scooted inside to her table. The teacher looked at me, a bit puzzled, but smiled and said thank you.

Angels speak through any mouth that works. I don't get to choose the timing of the lesson. It comes as it comes and it comes all at once on most days. Youth with age, sadness with joy, beginnings with endings. By asking her questions, this girl reminded me of something in my core — A heart big enough to hold a world full of opposites — and a mind capable of knowing they are one and the same.

If you ask a child what she was thinking when she yanked the braids off of her classmates —someone who just the day before was her best friend—she might give you a blank look. She wasn't thinking at all. I pile what children tell me into my brain and my heart and use an intuitive calculus to fill in the blanks. I have to guess at how close I have gotten to the truth.

2.

October

One Plus One

"Ever look at your face in the mirror?"
"Sometimes."
"Who do you see?"
"Well, I see me and. . ."
"And what?"
"When I look for a long time, I can see another person looking back at me."
"And who is that?"
"I don't know. Maybe it's another person that lives inside me. Or maybe it's the girl I want to become."

Dream

I am standing on a playground that resembles my school's yard — a flat asphalt square, wet, divided by the painted lines of play spaces. The blacktop sits adjacent to streets that pour downhill into alleys, apartments and a gathering mist.

I can't see the bay, but I feel it out there, beyond the fog. I say to myself that I must be dreaming. I have never seen fog as thick as this.

I am supervising dozens of fifth graders. But in dream truth, I am not in charge. Instead, I watch as children dart from the midst of roiling clouds. Each child emerges, walks past me, and makes no comment. They appear to have somewhere to go.

Since children are walking past me, I turn to see where they might be heading. I discover that the yard upon which I stand is called the middle yard and the place to which children climb, the upper yard. Only then do I also notice moss covered steps that rise into the same tumbling mist that hangs above everything. I can't see where the steps lead. Each child disappears and returns, a moment later.

"It won't let us through." A round-faced, gentle boy named Michael tells me. "It's blocking the way." Then a second child — a girl named Myra — returns with the same account. She stands before me with long black hair and black-rimmed glasses, large upon her small boned face. She shakes as she speaks: "I tried to go past, but a monster stopped me!"

I determine to climb the steps myself.

Into the clouds I go, finding myself stopped at the top of the stairs by a hairy beast so huge that I can see only its feet. I can smell its primordial must and can see that it stands so tall that it vanishes into the fog above me. I can't move it. I can't get past it, and I can't even get its attention. Then, the being makes a rumbling sound that shakes my bones. I, like the children, return to the middle yard.

On my return, I see a second set of steps that rise up from a lower yard. Has this third yard been here all along? A boy and girl ascend from below — the same two who spoke to me moments before. Myra, however, now carries a glowing sword, and Michael walks close beside her. With set faces, they nod as they pass. I watch them climb again to the upper yard.

With confrontation imminent, I follow.

I reach the top in time to see Myra raising her sword. Then I witness something else: two unlikely heroes engage a beast they can't see, in a battle without slashing, blood letting, or rending of flesh. Nothing but a roar rises up, *as if* Myra has made some fatal cut. The beast then divides into shimmering atoms. Atoms dissipate. Two ten year-olds stand to behold the threshold of what I know to be the upper yard — a yard now liberated for exploration.

The dream ends and the rest is mystery.

I stand watching boy and girl go forward and feel myself filling with an understanding: That courage is a potent weapon that can take down great beasts, and, that heroes are more powerful when they are less likely.

Second

At the end of recess last Friday, I blew the line-up whistle. The scramble began. It took only one child switching from walk to run and then the pandemic spread. In an instant I had twelve students dashing across the playground to be first.

Several boys showed remarkable cutting skills, slicing in front of their classmates from the side or doing the tried and true shove-and-cut. I sent the daredevils back across the yard and told them to try again,

"Walk all the way this time."

First place in line. First picked for kickball. First in the door. Coming in first, even in small ways, matters. Kids get this fact even if no one tells them so. So, the scramble for first is a matter of instinct, linked to the need to survive.

The more you come in first, the better you are thought to be. Fastest, smartest, strongest, most popular, most resourceful, and even meanest — all of these get their own forms of medals. Two recent examples reinforced this common perception:

Yesterday, a group of fifth graders in the after school program got invited to a pick-up soccer game with a school down the hill. Even before this no-stakes match, one of my students mentioned a boy named Enrique. He knew of him from the weekend league and the same name had come up in the parents' pre-game chatter.

I decided to watch the game.

"Mark him," I heard our coach say as the game started. I knew who he meant. Sure enough, the kid was fast. In a bit of a twist, the number 2 was embossed on his game jersey. And he was skilled! He dribbled the ball around the fullbacks, took out our players with slide tackles. We didn't have a chance.

His team won, 5 to 0. For this ten year-old, the scorecard no one kept would have held all of the required information.

So, what's this first-at-all-costs thing about when you break it down? What if the hunger for first place came from the fear of getting left behind. What if someone suggested that the long (and better) game was in learning how to navigate second? Who would buy that?

My guys, led by a serious and sweaty ten year-old named Benjamin, walked up the hill. All of our guys were quiet. "You guys did great." No comment. "You all never played as a team before." Silence. "We'll do a re-match next week."

"I don't care about losing." Benjamin spoke. "I just don't like Enrique. I hate it when he plays on the weekend, too, and he's on my team. He has to be first in everything."

Second isn't such a bad place to be. You get to learn about yourself when you have to endure a loss. You grow when you reach for the top but miss.

I want my kids to be civil. I ask them to pick up their fallen teammates and I teach them to say sorry when they are wrong. I am asking them to acquire the grace of second-place. I will bet that when they come back a second time, they are wiser, more intuitive, and maybe even more valuable to the rest of us.

May I suggest we celebrate second place, too? Victory comes from ruling over inside voices that tell us we're not good enough if we're not first. Think of the strength you need to get up, move on, be second and be strong!

Trap

From across the playground, I could see a pack of fourth graders encircling a boy named Tomas. They barked at him and he barked back.

"You're out, man. You're out."

"I'm not out. You lie."

Still more boys joined the ring around him, hollering. Tomas stuck to his post at second base. He stood in the middle of the painted square growing redder. Even when they took to calling him cry baby, telling him to go home or call his mom, he did not move. As I approached, I spat out some blunt commands.

"Back up. Move on. Game over."

Before I could get too close, however, Tomas ran. As he zipped off, I did a quick check-in with one of his classmates for the back story: someone threw a wobbly kick ball that smacked Tomas' backside. That smack knocked the non-event to an electric level. When Tobias figured out that the laughter had his name on it, he lost it.

As I went after him, I reviewed what I remembered from our previous encounters: tall kid, pale skinned, gifted in math, had a stutter, ran faster and showed more agility than many of the other boys. A myth followed him too; that he had once sling-shot a pigeon from the top of a telephone pole, dropping it to the ground. Most of all, however, I knew about his temper which other boys used to set him up weekly.

In the old monkey trap fable a critter slips his hand into a cage, grabs a banana, but, because he makes a fist, he can't get his hand free. And because he wants the banana, he will not relax the fist. For Tomas, this kind of trap played out when he had to back down. If he was wrong and got called on it, he could not yield.

And, he had stamina!

In the fable, the monkey dies. For Tomas, he would not quit. On five occasions, he stood in fist-clenched rage, refusing to vacate a base after he got tagged out.

"I'm not out. I'm not moving."

On this day, he had run toward an eight foot wall where he waited, fists clenched. I stepped between him and the wall, face-to-face. That's when I saw his eyes. Gray and clear as water. I could see in past the stubborn to someplace way inside this boy. Still, silent, and saying "Help!"

What next?

Traps cause critters to chew into their own soft tissue and draw blood as they struggle to pull free. The toughest come away scarred when they do come away. For this boy standing tall might take some chewing.

I kept him in my sights, stuck and strong, and felt him working through whatever went on inside. I stood there hoping he could see abundant mercy and graceful exits all around.

The hardest trap is the kind we set out for ourselves. In time, he yielded to tears. For tomorrow, still too soon to tell.

A bright spirit came in the body of a third grade girl. I saw her linger among second graders as they danced in a ring near the slide. She sat for a moment nearby, looking up and grinning as if to take it all in. Sunshine lit up her face. No place else she'd rather be!

Boat

I stood on the playground overlooking the Bay this morning. Four eight year-old boys stood with me. We were checking out the boats. Jaime looked up at me and asked:

"You ever been in a boat?"

"Yes I have,"

I told him about a time when I was eight where I went sailing with my father. We set out on a different bay in a small boat that could only hold the two of us. As I talked to Jaime, I could see my dad sitting in the stern with his life jacket on, grinning, and telling me to duck when the boom swung around.

I remember reaching over and putting my hand in the salt spray. Such a fast little boat. Then, I scrambled to the stern to watch the white water churn in the boat's wake. Hundreds of feet behind us, you wouldn't know our boat had come this way.

Back in the office an hour later, I got on a call from a friend of mine. Another principal who wanted to bail out. He told me he didn't have the energy to fight any more. Change is coming and I'm going to let it come. I had known him for eight years, and he was a no-nonsense fighter. He stuck it out. I told him about the boys, the bay, and the boat. You're the kind of man who stands up front, I said to him. Right in the wind. I don't know what I'm going to do without knowing you're there fighting on.

I remembered how it went when my dad died. We spent months planning, knowing he'd go, hoping he'd surprise us, get well, and be there to help make the next dream happen. Then life washed him overboard and I pretended nothing had happened. I kept pushing — staying busy, sailing into the storm. When I got off the phone with my friend, I understood what was happening. I didn't ask him too many questions. Water parts as we come through, and closes after we pass. We would continue, but not as we had.

Water swirls around movement. People, unlike water, tend to cling. I still have a boy in me that wants to start over, and wants to live forever so that I can keep trying new things. But everything changes. Even on a short trip in a sail boat, I might come back to a shore where things have shifted.

This morning, I got to dream with the boys about piloting big boats. This afternoon, I am sitting here among my lists of projects and tasks. My calendar shows dozens of one-on-one meetings aimed at making the odds break in our favor. Next to my desk hangs a clipboard complete with a check-list. And right now, I'm OK with letting most of it just wait. It can wait.

When I stood with the boys, looking out over the bay, a big puff of wind tumbled in. Even from the playground way up the hill, we could see sails grow taut. The boys and I watched as boats cut through choppy waters.

I thought of my dad grinning as he steered our tiny craft, and felt him again inside me even though he's long gone. No such thing as still water Dad used to say. Deep for sure. But never ever still. Today, I get what he meant. Do boats float forever? Jaime asked. Only till they sink my boy. That's the way it is.

Grudge

Jasmine is eight, round, and short. Her mother dresses her in fluorescent colors like hot pink, blinding orange, or way-too-lime green. None of this bright fabric can ever quite cover Jasmine's whole body. Her belly and back side seem to want (and find) a way out.

A couple of additional tidbits that complete the picture: Jasmine got dubbed "the fattest girl of all time" by a middle school boy who lived upstairs from her. He had tagged her with that name in kindergarten and it stuck. Her classmates, stocking stretchers in their own rights, picked up the label to harangue her each day.

The exchange came to a head when her cousin, Shareena, put skittles down the back side of Jasmine's pants as the girl bent down to pick up her lunch box. This unrequested drop-and-dash happened today.

I found Jasmine standing alone on the landing of the school's stairway. Her face was drenched from sobbing — she plucked the last of the bright skittles from the back of her hot pink pants. She approached me, leaned her wet face into my coat buttons, and came undone. "I hate Shareena. I am going to hate that little girl forever."

And so, a new grudge was born, joining a crowded field of old grudges and unfinished scores.

Grudges arise to protect us. However, grudges consist of dark, angry energy, wrapped tight and sourced through imprecise memories. "Getting even" lies tucked inside of every grudge as it hardens, grows, and leeches toxins into the psychic soil out of which new hopes and dreams can grow. Science can't quantify or even measure how these kinds of energies remain stuck in each of us. But any pair of open eyes can see the crush of the grudge on individuals as they shut down, become sour, and get mean.

You name the business, school, church or family, and grudges can accrue, choking the life out of the good work. Even small grudges cut through an organization's soft tissue, preventing healing, and blocking the ability for people to begin anew.

The blessing for me is to see my own barriers reflected in the children that I serve — along with the same humble tools needed in order to clear darkness and step closer to the realm of sweet light. Witnessing Jasmine clutching onto her memory of Shareena — I want her to find a way to let that memory go. Could it come from a thoughtful friend who might listen to her long enough to help her loosen the grip? Absent that kind of fortunate intervention, the world might shrink into a spiteful little place.

The catch is in how to step past the stuck-ness. I find the process to be slow going. For example, what if I happened to know a woman who held a grudge against me for ten years — and I against her. Let's say I found the strength to do the moral inventory, and then take the first step toward moving on. Let's even say that I had the audacity to make a phone call, to leave a message — an invitation to have a conversation over the phone to clear the air. All of these little actions would be part of finding my own inner hero.

Nothing changes when things stand still and leading may be about learning how to make things move. With that axiom in mind, I can see that I have work to do. Thank you, Jasmine, for getting things moving.

Front

Carlos stepped in front of me one day when I walked out onto the playground. Four feet tall with black hair slicked back, he stood his ground. He signaled for me to lean down. He had something important to tell me. Then, as I leaned, he reached up, fixed the knot in my tie and said to me — your pants and your tie — not happening. You're the boss man. You need to step it up! And don't worry. I got your back.

Wow. Really? I had been at my new school about a week — a brand new principal. Now this from an eight year-old. I took one look into this kid's big brown eyes and two things struck me. First, he meant it. Second, he meant well. He had sized me up and stepped in to help.

I checked out this pint-sized fashion plate and he had it together — shine on the shoes, pressed Ben Davis pants, white T-shirt, ironed. Precision and attention to detail. I got his point.

But I also felt as if I stuck out. Following that encounter, I got reminded of one of those "naked" dreams where one steps out on a big stage having left his costume backstage. I went through about sixty minutes feeling watched, hearing (and doubting) my own voice and second guessing even the simplest actions. Why had this stripping down not been included in my college courses? How about managing the feeling of having no place to hide.

I thought the edginess might ease, but instead, the sensation doubled up. I asked questions about my questions. I felt some of the raw stuff left over from boyhood coming back— this whole bit about being a leader or a follower — all of this within the first few hours on the job. I made a call to an old-time principal friend. She asked me how I was doing. She listened to my tone and said "hang in there" as she hung up.

Exposure — the imposter feeling — doesn't kill you. I know that now. Likewise, sitting in a circle, talking about leadership does little to prepare anyone for the body blows that come along with the job. If you do survive the journey from theoretical to factual, you have to come to terms with all of those "incompletes" — the myths about manhood, the lies, and the battering that comes from perpetual public review.

From above, I hear this: I am capable, I am kind, I am fragile, and I am who I am.

Eloise Brookes, a take-no-prisoners leader who had a formative impact on my early leadership years, had long lived in the public eye. She told me that everyone deserves the dignity of privacy. But when you go, then go. Don't be standing out there, looking all surprised. You'll just make a fool of yourself.

So, Carlos remains my adviser. I carry his memory in my lapel pocket, I check my ties twice and make sure that my belt and shoes match. And, no matter how much attention I place on the look, I know that there's no point in holding back. In the end, all that I am is all that I ever had to give. I have to be good with that.

That fear that someone will put one over on me lives in the back of my brain. The same place where fighting and fleeing live. If I stay there, my days become endless, exhausting and unforgiving. To move forward in a new way this time around, even if I can't see the way. How do I generate the kind of magic that will keep me from getting stuck?

Bones

Two days ago, I came upon Shelby, a seven year old, standing in the doorway to the social worker's office. I drew closer and could see her scuffed high-tops (one untied), a backpack crumpled beside her, and her teeth biting into her lower lip. She clenched both fists and let forth a whimpering sound — a soft wail that issued from her bones.

I asked the social worker — where did you find her? In front of the school. What else can you tell me? Nothing — she hasn't said a word. How long has she been here? We have both been here for the past ten minutes. What should we do? I don't know. Did you call home? I left a message? Well?

I've called her mom. She's coming. We just have to wait. We just have to wait.

The social worker dropped her pencil onto the desktop. She pushed back from her desk. The three of us waited the way we might wait on any given day, wishing for a tactic or insight that might snap us forward to some new undiscovered place called 'whatever comes next.' Then the room became still.

A tall woman, dark, calm, appeared at the top of the stairs. I hadn't seen her before but I knew who she was. She approached and I stepped aside. Leaning down, she said nothing more than 'hush', and planted a kiss on the little girl's braids. Shelby looked up toward her mother's face and their eyes met.

Get to class. I'll bring your lunch. Everything's going to be alright.

Magic between the words that will never appear in any spell. Gentle, deep, and silent transmission between these two spirits. They sufficed. Shelby picked up her backpack and left on her own. Then, mom and social worker stepped out. I remained.

Behind me the door locked. In that solitude, silence gathered. I could not speak to what lay in that silence. I could feel an ache that the little girl had left behind — as if she left it for me to consider.

Shelby's mother rubbed ointment and heated through to the marrow. She righted things the way a mother can. She soothed the rawness and reminded her daughter that she would be there for her. Her kiss stilled the little girl; communion that connected through emptiness. She reminded me of my mother's kiss that could still lift my spirit these many years later.

Everything will be alright.

Wisdom waits within the bones. It comes forth when it has to. That arising might come without warning and I know of no way to prepare for it. Bones, for their part, waste no time on the cumbersome ways of spoken words. Be still, be still, be still. Have your dream and pretend. Lean into a storm, tight jawed and fearless.

Then release the dream and let emptiness fill with softer truths. Let all of it in this second time through. Say less. Hear more. Be as strong as your child's heart allows. That will be enough.

Quiet

Over the weekend, I rode with family on a stretch of road that runs along the edge of a cemetery. On both sides, old maple trees tossed in the wind and dropped thousands of leaves. I had a quiet moment where I followed a single leaf as it descended in crescents until it came to rest on wet grass. We drove past and moved on.

This morning, Monday, I watched as sixteen lines of school children, waited for their teachers to take them indoors on this windy day. They pulled their collars up and shoved their hands in pockets. Then, line by line, teachers descended from the upper floors, raised quiet signals, and beckoned the lines to come. Noises fell to whispers. Quiet extended its pale palm across the entire playground. Only a truck engine grinding up the hill just beyond the projects roared and grew fainter with distance.

Just now, I stepped into my office out of the noisy halls. I closed the door. Then, a hush poured in, made more complete by concrete walls of this old cinder-block school. A shift in consciousness came in that instant after sudden silence — and timid notions, tucked in my mind's nooks, began to spill out. They had been waiting, so silence slipped away in the noise of my mind. In moments like these, I write these notes.

Top of mind is a day that begins with silence. And if not the whole school, I imagine my own twelve year old standing on the back stoop all by himself — beginning his day with an inward moment. Not silence as a formal or complex thing. Such complexities are their own form of noise. Instead, I think about starting a day on purpose — a revolutionary act that comes without a single cannon blast or shout.

Quiet arrives in stages just as it did this morning on the playground. Then, it deepens when you notice it and allow its spell to drop deeper inside. Past that, the journey into stillness comes through practice. You have to seek it and engage the practices that allow it to carry you in. By degrees, you find that even seeking quiet as a goal is its own kind of sound. Silence at this stage becomes more about permission than a push.

When noise rises on the playground, it creates pressure. Pressure distorts. Distortion bends perception and when truth bends enough, it becomes an unintended lie. A day of complete peace, a disappearance of aggression, or even the forced arrival of any uninvited agenda — all of these kinds of noise create pressure.

Even as I pause before dropping in to this day, I can hear a kind of predictive cacophony in what might be — shoving its way to the fore of my mind, announcing itself, and shoving its way in a manner unique to undesired noise. It will pull me away from where and how I want to be.

So the day begins.

No absolute silence exists except within a vacuum and very few of us ever experience the kind of quiet that can occur there. Later, may I find time to let the noise drain out through the soles of my feet, into the concrete floors and then down into the earth itself. I seek to know how to allow myself to become quiet, quiet, quiet. . .What next surprise waits to open within me?

Flash

A flash in the form of a three foot, nine inch boy lit up the yard this morning. I hadn't witnessed a pure blue bolt quite like this one before. Now, I find myself standing here, in the middle of the empty kickball diamond, scribbling notes. My question: What did I see? I don't want to let the details slip away even if one can't capture everything with pen and paper. Here's what I know:

He arrived new to the school just three days ago. Today, I learned his name: Amir. When I spotted him this morning, I couldn't tell much other than the fact that he wanted to get away from mom. She plodded several feet behind the father, carrying the boy. A short distance ahead of mother and son, the boy's father strolled, tall, proud, accustomed to big steps. He surveyed the blacktop with a king's confidence. Protective. In charge.

Amir and mom, meanwhile, continued to wrestle. He would not be denied! With a last kick, he broke free, landing on the asphalt with a two-footed thud. Then, he ran forward several feet, stopped, dropped to his knees, reached toward his father and shouted:

"Dad! Wait!"

The urgency in his cry woke me up! How could such a sound, notches above every other noise on the playground, emanate from such a small boy? And as the blue bolt of this child's plea flashed, I caught the eyes of several other fathers, looking at me as I looked back. Amazement? Affirmation? Confirmation?

So, how to explain the curious shift that came next? An instant where the fathers on the playground noticed one another, united by whatever the boy had released. All of us — brown, black, white, young, old, moved closer. Non-verbal but palpable — linked — boy to father, father to grandfather, back and back even as far as some long forgotten beginning.

Men don't often get along on the world's open stage. We fight, compete, rip upon each other, and make gains at the expense of our brothers. When an exception occurs, I ask how could we have come to this different place? Were we not born to separateness? Might there be another choice? Amir's dad, at least pertaining to his son, required no further instruction. As the boy ran toward father, dad turned, opened his arms and received. Amir jumped up and his father caught him, placing him on his right hip. The two went forward as one.

For me, I am standing here scribbling in an afterglow: I saw one brilliant flash across a cloudy, unremarkable morning. In that light, I could approximate the worlds inside of other people. The moment became a tableau apart from time. It marked where and how we stood. That light that erased margins and scrubbed away boundaries. And then it fell back to its former dull gray.

A moment, real as the boy's place at his father's side. I don't have a thousand hours or enough ink to unfurl every minute detail. We toss such tidbits aside as if they were trifles. Now, an essential simplicity shone upon me. I could have had my back turned and missed everything. Instead, strangers connected across differences by way of the heart.

Let that be all for now. For me, that's more than I need.

Flower

In front of me stood a breathless, upset, ten year-old, Daffnee. Teary eyed, she bobbed up and down, over-sized beret flopping with each spoken fragment. Words fell out in fives and tens. As she'd come near to completing a thought, she'd get stuck and head back for one more go.

I waited as her lips trembled and she collected herself.

Not that the girl held back much on any given day. She tended to over-share and, in truth, kept few personal details to herself. Today's chant, however, had a different urgency.

If I could only get her to make sense.

"I can see you're upset, sweetheart. Sit down and take a breath." She plunked down next to me on a concrete stoop along the playground's east side. Recess would start soon. I hoped to squeeze her story out beforehand so that I would know what we might need to sort out. I did not expect it to be anything big, but something was clearly amiss.

Half way through another attempt to speak, her voice hitched, and she surrendered, letting her head land with a clunk on my shoulder. At that moment, I intuited something bigger than sadness. More of a red-eared burn that I associate with shame. "Take your time, dear. Talk to me when you're ready."

Daffnee could not get the story out but another voice did pipe in. "I can tell y'all what happened."

Daffnee's cousin, Keena, had been observing as Daffnee struggled. Cousin watched but could no longer wait. In a few blunt sentences, she laid out the pertinent facts: Daffnee's big-armed teacher, Ms. Milversted, had made her stand up in front of thirty classmates while teacher then informed child that she'd "never get anyone to respect your mind if you come to school dressed like an Oompa Loompa."

With Daffnee now sobbing, Keena spoke for her cousin once more: "I don't know what's up, principal. I don't even know what a Oompa Loompa is. But that's just wrong. My cousin never hurt nobody! And look at her now. Teacher or not, how that old woman go on and get so mean that way?"

Excellent question. One I would need to investigate. But first, Daffnee would need to get patched up. Then I'd figure out how to mop up the rest.

I saw a tough young advocate in Keena, ready to see truth and call it out. She left me to consider a swirling set of questions. For example: How can grown folks learn — or maybe remember — when to salt and when to salve? And will we ever learn how to treat one another with kindness? Could we find a way to pour our mis-speaks, mis-steps and mistakes into one shared cup — and could we know to go to this cup before we made our next moves? Or will we go on repeating ourselves, slipping, regretting, wishing, after the fact, that we'd done things another way?

As the flower in a young girl's soul blooms, fragile and transcendent beauty reveals itself. It may show up in something she chooses to wear, in a poem she reads out loud, or even in a lingering look that she gives at the end of a conversation. Poke at it with salt-tipped remarks and you can kill a bloom outright. I heard Keena's words becoming my own: "That's just plain wrong."

To learn, grow, and carry the heart of that learning forward. That's the challenge that appears to demand my attention here, and in the weeks ahead.

3.

November

What Comes of This?

"How come you guys are so quiet?"
"We ran out of stuff to talk about."
"Hmm. Really?"
"It's cool. Sometimes we just can't think of anything to say."
"So what are you going to do now?"
"We're gonna go hang out by the fence and watch the boats."
"Then what?"
"Something will happen. Something always happens."
"OK, let me know."
"We're gonna surprise you."
"I can't wait."

Stand

Kids from the neighborhood, when they first come to school, bring along their street-ruled games. First rule: Stay in until you can't. As long as you can stand, you can play. Last long enough and you become a neighborhood titan.

Isaiah — or Isaiah the Thin — was one such titan who could have quit long ago. He had a mouth that never stayed shut, jeans that never stayed up and a big-boy swagger that came on stronger than his eighty pounds warranted. However, yesterday, when Kuma'je — Kuma'je the Large — flattened Isaiah the Thin, we thought that would be that.

A crunch from across the yard caught my ear. I turned to see Isaiah face down, left shoe missing, shirt torn, pants yanked. A complete wipe out. In every previous clash, even if he got dropped, he popped up, cursed, did a few circles of show-time limps, and then returned to the games. This time, a little ring of boys had gathered around. None stooped to pick him up. When I got there, they spat out excuses, whom to blame and so on. Isaiah made not a sound.

I stooped down to check for vital signs and he opened his eyes — good — made eye contact with me — better. I reached in to help him get up but no — I can do this he said. — and he made as if to stand under his own power. Far from steady, rise he did. He yanked his shirt around, cranked his jeans back up, eyed his scrapes — and caught a shoe one boy tossed him. The circle of boys stepped back. Only the sound of the bell stopped him from going at it again.

When I watch these kids play, I understand their games have high stakes. Failing to stand up serves as proof that they can't take it. If they can't take it, then they don't count. So, even when they should not, they step to the games again. Their resolve takes me back to times where I played on — and others where I quit. Quitting leaves behind questions: What if I had stood up one more time? Would things have turned out some other way?

When (If) Isaiah grows to adulthood, he will not be a big man. He comes from a long line of rail thin men, none of whom tops five-eight, 150 pounds. At some point, he will need to come to terms with his pint size. Given the company he keeps, he may have to find his own way forward when he gets taken down. He shows me a few new tricks that can help me make the best of a good wipe out — how to find that hidden strength that allows me to stand when I thought I no longer could.

Isaiah might be like heroes of old who set out on long journeys full of pride and returned humbled by mistakes, wizened, and stronger thereby. For him and for me, we go through this grind on a hunch that it will lead to better ends. Since we're both still standing, we have not only risen from each trip-and-fall, but also returned for another round a touch more reflective — and maybe a bit better for it all.

As long as the pains bring these kinds of gains, I'm still in.

Grape

I sat across from a row of kindergarten boys in the lunchroom today. They came skidding in along the linoleum and then went piling onto bench seats. I watched as they popped open lunch boxes. All of them waved but they didn't want to talk. Time to eat!

I knew most of their names as they were already becoming regulars in the front office. For example, shaved-head Henry who brought lunch in a drawstring bag. He dumped everything out: Apple slices, cheese wedges and salami. And the quiet boy, Gordon, who pried back the lid of a long plastic container to get at nine sushi-styled rice blocks, each topped in a dash of green and red.

But my eyes landed on Wyman, a square-jawed five year-old, who sat still without a trace of a smile. He focused on his red lunch sack from which he pulled two plastic tubs, one containing a quartered sandwich, and a another that held a bunch of shiny, plump grapes, still on stem.

What I noticed was the precision in his movements: slow centering of tub to its rightful place in front of his scrunched face. He used a two-fingered technique for pulling off the lid. Stop, study, adjust, tug.

So what next?

From the way Wyman scanned the tub's contents, I knew he sought a particular grape in mind. Spotting it, he plucked his prize, held it between thumb and forefinger, extended his arm away from his face and then brought the shiny morsel in for a landing on the cradle of his extended tongue. His lips closed like doors to a vault.

We both waited.

Wyman took one more pause. Then came the crush. His eyes rolled back. I could tell when he chomped down because his mouth twisted and his shoulders shuddered. I got to watch an entire being come to terms with a small explosion of juice and pulp. And throughout, he kept his mouth closed, remaining immersed in this moment, giving over to sweet sensation. He and the grape became one.

Believe me when I tell you this:

Long ago, above and below were joined. Then, the minds of men began to assign names to all things. As their strength grew, they ranked circumstances and dismissed entire days as if they were non-essential. Very little of the essence of things survived. Tangible and intangible became divided into parts. We lost much when this change came on us.

But today, juice rolling over the tongue, sliding down the throat — such a splendid event had to be taken whole-as it was for Wyman whose every cell became one with the grape. No quibbling about what to call what. Just the primacy of singular experience and an unimpeded encounter with ineffable wholeness.

Children remind me that the points between the named things are the ones I must not forget. That's the prize. To catch these moments when they come along, cradle them on the tongue, slow way, way down, and let them enter in their inexplicable, overwhelming totality. Wisdom must come through the absence of an explanation.

Be still, says Thích Nhất Hạnh, and know — like children who can bring us back home, and can also in their effortless ways, return us to the point of contact — where above and below have a chance to become one once again.

Home

Most mornings, I see eight-year old Jermayne as he arrives on the playground. He comes through the big gates, takes a single step onto the yard and then stops. Every day he stops on the same spot. He lifts his chin, looks straight ahead, and forms an X with his index fingers. Holding this X held in front of his face, he advances a few yards, marks a spot, proceeds, marks, stops —repeat. As he walks from point to point, he hums.

Jump back to two weeks ago. The boy and I came face-to-face as he marked out an almost empty yard. I waited in the center, tracking his angles east — stop — X, then west — stop — X. Then he came my way. In front of me he stopped, avoided eye contact because that's not something he does, marked the spot- X and snapped his fingers twice.

Before he stepped away, I asked — where are you going? Home, said he. Just a single word. Then, he started humming and commenced to the next X. In that little moment, I saw not only how Jermayne's searching worked — but also why.

Marian, a principal mentor from my earlier years in leadership once talked to me about how to find your way when you get lost. "Listen with big ears. Listen all the way in and don't be so eager to talk all the time. We lead better when we use our ears more and our mouths less. Secrets whisper in from quieter places and not so much from the loudest mouth or the fastest talker. If you start to drift, try listening this way. You'll like what you find out."

My thoughts about Jermayne and Marian came up again yesterday as I sat at a table with a group of super smart folks, board members, talking about their organization's mission, vision, and values. They got to arguing about particular words, the order of phrases, where to put commas, and which verb had more punch.

I offered a story about stepping out onto my back deck the night before to look at the stars. What a night! Cloudless, cold, windy. Distant points of light popped and it seemed I could see even ringed planets turning. I felt myself as one of those small points, tiny, but connected to it all. If your words are stars, you have all the words you need. Consider them all together. Not one by one. That's how you'll know. They grinned and continued arguing, but that's how it goes. I went back to listening.

Home has little to do with particulars like a plot of land, a building, or a knapsack tossed under a bridge. It comes from a unity that happens on the inside. Finding it comes from making the journey — X to X, not from sticking to one point. I once told a group of fifth graders, for example, to grab hold of those wandering times. They'll teach you what to do when you wander off track.

I am still journeying. I listen into the speechlessness of wanderers like Jermayne. It speaks to hidden parts within me. Such places need patience and quiet to come back out. I can't tell anyone what he should do. I can, however, share what I know about marking X's and moving on. If the deepest listening will ever come, times where I haven't a clue are the moments I have to look forward to.

When I come face to face with a human storm, do I duck? How can I stand in the wind and blow it back? I have to make peace with the storms. To get wet is part of it and it may reveal more about how to serve.

Bridge

When seven year-old Raymond came to school each morning, he had to walk only a few blocks. He came by way of three alleys and a set of stairs. Not too far maybe, but farther than forever on some days. I once asked him, do you ever get scared coming to school by yourself. He flipped back his brown hair and said "What the heck! Come on."

Not scared, Raymond? Ever? Fair enough, I said.

He made his way up hill this morning and from my window, I could see him reaching the gate. I could also *hear* him singing a loud, out of key tune sincere as a spit-shined shoe.

Then it came to me that today was Tuesday, the day Mr. Tee comes to Raymond's classroom. He brings guitar, kind eyes, and a gentle voice that infuses peace into everything he touches. I see him as a kind of bridge — one who uses music to carry kids from this world to the next and back. Raucous Room 103, for example, became home to harmony when Tee was there. However he did it, I felt grateful.

Today, I said to myself, I'm going to sit in a while and sing along with the kids. So, I wrapped up a couple of desktop details, grabbed my keys, and headed downstairs. The school would be fine without the principal for a few minutes! Just a little break to sit and take in some of the magic. And from the moment I stepped in, I knew that Tee would not disappoint:

"If I play a note here" he plucked air with thumb and forefinger of left hand "and then I play a second note there" he plucked the air again, now with right hand,

"what do you think fills in all that space between those two notes?"

"Just air! There's nothing there!" Raymond shouted first.

"Just air Raymond? You sure?" Tee picked up his guitar, rested it on his knee, and began to pluck notes as he continued his story. "Close your eyes. Let your ears hear everything. What I play, and even what I don't. Can you hear everything? Even what you thought was no sound at all?"

Instead of closing his eyes, Raymond's eyes widened as Tee went on:

"When you pluck a note, you set it free. No matter how far it travels, it will find its way home. When a note splits in half, quarters or eighths, it's still part of the same family. One day, every single quarter and half will find its way to the great whole in the sky." Tee stood up for a moment, grinning, as he rumbled through six chords, three times, just to prove his point.

Kids bowed and bent like blades of grass as they followed his song. No matter how far his strumming roamed, he plucked back to where it all began.

Children sang out and I joined in. A room full of hearts that didn't care what the words meant. I got to watch Raymond riding songs the way a sharp rides a flat, sweeping up, hanging on, sliding back home by way of the bridge. He vanished into a far bigger song that came alive in that classroom. In the music, he let himself go. In letting himself go, he let himself be.

Song ended, and I headed out with thanks to one and all! When had I ever heard music better than that?

35

Hiding

Story time in the library. Ms. O'Reilly had just read the part where the little princess, missing for days, had been seen floating downstream on a skiff piloted by an ill-intended reptile — a scaly critter with unwholesome plans for the princess' long lockets. Then, a call came in over the loud speaker. Something had come up. Time to snap to.

I learned that two girls, Ana and Emily, last seen chatting in morning circle and tapping their pretty-kitty shoes along playground fence posts, had disappeared. Their absence turned up in the first head count of day.

Since kindergartners are small, they can hide in plenty of places — tucked inside closets, locked in bathroom stalls, stuffed under playground benches, I dispatched every available staff person to search. We looked everywhere.

As a rule, we allow no more than ten minutes before calling local officers for support. I had the phone in my hand when a red-faced aide ran in to tell me she had found both girls — coiled and giggling inside two big tractor tires that serve as our school's tire swings.

I lined both of them up, told them they had scared us by hiding, and leaned in to make an impression. However, even as I finger-wagged them, they played with their ringlets. Maybe I was losing my touch? I made a note to call their moms and sent them back to class. Later, they became the talk of the playground.

Come the second day, I got a repeat. I stood at my desk, shuffling through while-you-were-out slips and Enrique, age five, entered. He stood in the center of the room, arms folded, brows furrowed, jacket collar turned up.

I am missing, he told me. No you are not, I answered. You are right here.

He said he had been hiding for a whole hour, in the janitor's closet with all the mops and buckets. Mr. Carpenter had turned out the light and closed the door.

I been in the dark and nobody came.

With Enrique in tow, I bolted toward his classroom. There, Ms. Gladys, a substitute of almost seventy, held court with a circle of children who listened to her read about the fox and the swan.

I marked him absent sir. He never made it to class, I'm sorry.

I had to stop and reflect for a moment. Could it be that this little boy had decided to put the big people through a drill? He stood at my side, still brow-furrowed, scratching at his shaved head, surveying his classmates, me and his substitute teacher.

You looked for the girls. No one came for me. I could have died.

I found myself unable to speak. I told him to sit down. Then I left the room.

Everyone needs to be seen. Most of us get ignored much of the time. Such is life. I need to pay attention to little messengers. Surprises come obscured behind loud noises and sparkling urgencies. I should be about looking, even when nothing seems lost. I have no way to account for what I may have missed. Better to see that I have no time to waste.

Pretend

Pretending creates a dividing line — real as a rock on one side, paired with somewhat squishier realities on the other. I used to think I knew where to draw that line, but I used to think a lot of things. Today during morning recess, my thoughts got a shove from a third grade boy named Khalil.

Recess started with a tag game — chasing, hiding, and time-outs, the usual. Then, the game kicked up a notch when two of the boys claimed they could fly. Another said he could freeze people with just a touch. Game on! To the top of the play structure, under benches, behind a row of shrubs.

A few broke off from the rest to build a fort. On it went.

Meanwhile, on this side of the time-space continuum, recess came to a close. Ms. Keith rang the hand bell. Kick balls whooshed into ball bags, lines formed behind line leaders, and the playground fantasia approached the final notes.

Then, I saw Khalil.

This brown-eyed dreamer stayed twenty feet from the next nearest child, high-kicking and low-punching invisible phantoms, blocking unseen jabs from the left and right. At last he froze in his ready stance, facing me. Ms. Keith approached, scooting him away from his flying foes and down steps, toward the building.

I walked part of the way to his classroom and saw that even indoors Khalil did not re-integrate. Ms. Keith whispered calming closers: Of course dear. Oh my. How scary. Shush, shush. They're all gone now. I'm glad you're back. She winked at me as she closed her classroom door.

So much for Khalil's little adventure.

My teachers used to call me a day dreamer. And even though they meant the label as a dunning, my mother backed me up. She told a family story about my grandmother who had visions now and then. She was one powerful pretender, my mother explained. In her visions, she traveled everywhere.

She crossed seas, learned secrets, knew spells, and chanted to the invisible. The longer the journey, the better the ride — her only rule.

Sometimes, the things that grandmother saw had a way of coming true. "Just remember that, honey. You might be like her."

Where teachers wanted to tether me — "Pay attention! You'll never go anywhere dreaming!" — I wanted to fly, to meet people with visions like mine, and to see beyond seeing. I sought confirmation from somewhere — anywhere. At night, I lay flat and stared into the starry vastness. I watched for signs. Was someone out there trying to reach me? How would I know for sure?

In that instant when I stood face-to-face with a boy accused of practicing an excess of make-believe, my boyhood came back. I faced myself and wondered how much Khalil had already figured out. Did he have anyone to talk to or did he carry his visions all alone?

Yes, Khalil, I want you to pay attention, but to what *you* see. Not so much what you're told to see. Seek, get lost, dream and discover. You might come back empty handed. But you might return with an answer or two, connections we had failed to see, or tales of the bold, uncanny realms on the other side of the line.

Be brave and go far. Hopes rely on wonders that at first only a dreamer sees.

Twins

If you look up on a clear night, you might be able to pick out twin stars dancing in perpetual round-about. Two weeks ago, I came to know two such stars, captured in the skinny bodies of Diana and Evangeline — inseparable fifth grade girls.

Their two teachers talked about them during yard duty — they don't seem to fit with anyone else. Then I got a chance to meet Diana (without Evangeline) during parent-teacher conferences. That encounter proved to be the beginning of a tale about friends, bullies, and heroes.

I found out that Diana never missed school. She also liked to draw. Flowers, faces, exploding stars, and cats. During our conference, Diana drew as her parents mentioned the other girl, Evangeline. Parents asked that I keep the two girls apart. They don't bring out the best in one another, said the father.

Three days after this conference, I learned more from my school social worker. She explained that she had been working with Diana since kindergarten. The kids teased her. Merciless. But she and Evangeline did not seem to notice.

Now, enter the bully — a squat boy with a chipped tooth. Maynard (the kids called him Round Face). He led other fifth graders in a game called Cheese Touch. In this game, he who is Cheese Touched becomes outcast until he passes thetouch on to someone else. Once I learned of the game, I saw cheese everywhere. I saw kids playing it everywhere. How had I missed it? And, just as my social worker had told me, there were no bigger cheeses than Diana and Evangeline.

I gathered all the students from the upper grades last Friday and banned the game. Then it went underground.

At the start of the second week, I saw how the twin stars stuck with each other. They saw no one else and did not know the swirl surrounding them. Regardless, the game came to a head in a surprising way just yesterday. From across the yard, I saw Maynard attaching a stuffed white glove to the end of a stick. He dangled it over Evangeline and Diana. They remained oblivious. Neither girl even looked up. To them, they were alone together.

I hustled from the kickball court toward the basketball hoop — a hundred yard journey. Meanwhile, Round Face pressed on. Even without Diana and Evangeline's participation, he raised the glove over his head, shouted 'Diana Touched' and swung it around. Then came a surprise.

Maynard smacked (on accident) Little Maya. Big mistake. This short-haired fireplug grabbed the boy's stick, snapped it, and then snagged his glove. She touched herself all over. "You wanna touch something, touch summa this."

Maya cornered Maynard and shoved the glove in the boy's mouth. The twin stars made another quarter turn, jump rope re-started, and three third graders ran back to the monkey bars for another go at getting across.

Playgrounds deliver with efficiency. Painful, but quick justice. Helpless dreamers prevail. Cowards get crushed. Since I saw it on the blacktop, I have faith that it can happen anywhere.

Diana and Evangeline.

Naked

Before you ever reach your grown-up, rule-following, upstanding citizen of a self, you begin with an original self. On the receiving end, an original self can deliver one hot mess. As if I needed more proof, I had a moment with one such self, Damien, last Tuesday.

Damien sported a flat-side haircut, and more space than teeth in his mouth with remaining teeth capped in silver. He had two deep brown eyes that swam in their sockets. Once he looked up at me and declared I am one crazy boy.

A month ago, I went into his classroom during free choice time. Kids could draw, play with blocks, and dress up. Damien popped out — tah-dah — from the shoe cubby wearing a wedding veil, a hoop skirt, and earrings made of scotch tape and red construction paper. How you like these earrings Principal? They nice, don't you think?

Nice, I said. Nice.

On Tuesday, when I heard his way-too-happy tee-hee-hee, I stepped into the hall to see him pop through the door of his kindergarten classroom, kick off his orange-and-scrunge shoes, drop his jeans *and* his polka dot drawers, and run naked down the blue-tile floor that extended from the south end of the hall to the north. Away went his two brown buns bouncing, fast, and disappearing down the school's back steps. I snatched pants, shorts, shoes, and walkie-talkie and began the pursuit.

Picture Damien. Then step back to think about how we build schools. Rows of concrete boxes tethered to the sides of long, shiny-slick hallways. Hallways are also boxes, albeit long and narrow. Whether stacked or stretched long ways, these cubes still have just a few cut-outs that that allow their human cargo outward and onward toward any available light. The laughter of children echoes within them, gets caught, falls to the floor, and dims. I do not know how we chose to make schools this way. Maybe we will change our ways.

If a boy gets caught here, he can sometimes make it out. He has to figure out patience, how to say yes when he wants to say no, how to sweet-smile, and how to sit still.

I caught up with him, holding naked court on the playground for a ring of fourth grade girls and boys. He got to be in the center of creation for that glorious, wide open moment. One of the yard supervisors, Ms. Angus, snagged him by the arm and pulled his pants back on his squiggly body. I could see how this moment worked her nerves as she buttoned his jeans and tugged his red-cloth belt a notch too tight.

Now was when he would start his lesson — the one about staying indoors, being a good boy, a quiet boy who knows to keep pants on and his eyes down. As Ms. Angus took him upstairs, I heard her saying, you should have thought about that, little boy, before you took off down that hall.

So, ask yourself what happens when a boy escapes? When he gets out without knowing how to run, where to go, where to get help? We don't yet have that answer and are still doing the research Damien.

For now, lay low.

Freedom shows itself in people who give without measure. Through serving others rather than in how to make others useful. Transformation happens when leaders break free of their own greatness. We matter when we don't. Both are true. What we trade in loving children gives more than it takes.

Walk

What happens when a seven year old boy walks out of a classroom and refuses to stop? Or when he runs across a playground toward the high chain link fence? Picture his black hair, bowl-cut, bangs just a half inch above the eyebrows, brown eyes shining out from the darkness of his face. Thin jacket, thin frame. Then comes wind and rain along with the voice of a teacher shouting "get back here this instant."

He climbs the fence, over and down to begin a determined march to a point unknown. Grownups scramble to respond, but in the seven minutes it takes to get organized, we fear that anything might happen. He heads toward alleys between apartments across the street. These alleys are known for random gunfire and illicit transactions.

Within him, something wants to find center. It becomes my responsibility to bolt after him, snag him by the hood of his thin jacket, turn him around, and march him back to the school. As he squirms, he gets a loud lecture about the knuckle-headed prank he just pulled. I ask him, where did you plan to go? Over the bridge? And then where? I conclude with something like — you have no idea!

His vision quest will have to wait.

When I tell my friend Puanani Burgess about boys like this one, she wants me to share more. OK, so he is stubborn and won't speak to you. What else? He scares you when he runs off. I understand. Now, tell me this. If I put it to you, could you name even one of his gifts? What do you know about him? I'm putting it to you right now. Tell me something about him other than how he makes you feel.

She has worked for years with families on the Hawaiian island of Oahu in the town of Waianae. Lots of hard journeys but lots of cloud breaks, too. She has plenty of stories about kids like mine, setting off angry and confused, no inkling of what drives them out and no clue about where they might be heading. She might tease me by asking — so what would happen if you didn't stop him? Could you keep him safe, but still just let him go?

I know that I can't. I stop little boys all the time when they get steam-headed ideas to head out on their own. I know they are not ready for the big walks, but I also know they will not become ready until they fall. Truth is strong medicine, but too much, too soon, can kill. I see how these points conflict.

When I see him next week, his need to walk will remain. And the moment — the right moment — will have to wait, patient, quiet. Then, he will some day step out, no one to stop him. The less he holds back, the more efficient the truth will be in providing a complete lesson. Nothing will be wasted. So my big wish for him is that his walk may bring him beginnings of courage, wings that unfold, or maybe just a simple chance to know how lucky he is to be able to walk in such a remarkable, ineffable time.

Touch

When a child snaps and freefall begins, you can learn a lot from the ensuing scramble. Arturo, an eight year old, showed that he had snapped last week when he punched and bit a couple of child crisis staff, scrawled swear words on the office wall, and kicked at the air to scare the rest of us away. During it all, I witnessed more than a child in crisis.

I also saw how guidelines and procedures fail to chart how we should behave when we slip outside of the situations the guidebooks' authors anticipated. For example, at one point, a frustrated social worker pulled the crisis manual from the shelf to see what she must have missed. She set it down in seconds. We were off script. Two staff restrained the boy and at that point we went somewhere beyond the warning that says, above all else, do not touch.

Touching, as essential as it is, is also tricky. The rule is to touch only when all else has been tried. The nature of how touch occurs is described, regulated and sometimes inadequate. When Arturo fled, staff had been using approved holds. Still, he slipped free and ducked down hallways to hide.

Police officers arrived, found him in a custodial closet, and coaxed him back to my office. We stood together, a room full of experts baffled by how to contain the uncontainable. One large social worker cornered Arturo behind a desk while case workers and staff worked the phones seeking clearances and guidance from their superiors. They got voicemail. One officer relented and said let's pick him up.

They lifted Arturo, one on each arm, dragged him across the street and stuffed him, kicking and swinging, into the back of a squad car.

One of my bosses once described events beyond the limits of our systems — untouchable places where irregular circumstances wait. This same boss told us that a requisite for leadership was a willingness to step into that untouchable, unchartered place to foster the connections that systems refuse to. He outlined case after case where rulebooks could only take you so far, and then you had to move ahead without the support of precedent, a clear map, or an encouraging word.

His words brought to mind a time of a very different moment, when a former President stood between two quarreling Middle East leaders during negotiations, taking one man's hand and joining it with the other in a hand shake. News lines buzzed with this president's audacious act. He had stepped over a line in introducing touch. No script, but instead, powerful impact and for a moment, a bit of hope.

We earned our broken and battered retreat to touchless interventions through many abuses. Melt downs and collapses are an unpredictable expectation, and sometimes all we can do is to stand by, helpless. That we might relearn now to listen to the body, and how to re-engage the power of simple contact — do we have to make it so challenging for reliable wisdom to work its magic? As the pace of free fall quickens we may want to revisit what we thought we knew.

4.

December
Two Times Two

"Come on! You wastin' my time!"
"Hey, Sara! Why are you yelling?"
"We just standing around out here."
"What else you gonna do?"
"I got stuff to do."
"Like what?"
"Like stuff. I don't have time to stand in this line."
"Those girls are slowing things down."
"They think they cute but they ain't."
"Take a breath. You'll be OK."
"Oh my god."
"Breathe, Sara. Easy does it."

Middle

I am having another dream. I am half way down the slide on my school's playground. Nine children want to slide down, and nine want to climb up. I am in the middle.

Smaller children squint and begin getting squished from the downward pressure. I yell to the boy at the top, a loud and screaming boy named Hernando, that he should back up. "You are crushing us." I say. He can't hear me.

I yell at a stout, strong-armed girl named Luciana that she should stop trying to climb up. "Go down the slide! We are getting squished." She grins and redoubles her efforts to shove her way up the slide.

"Come on! Stop! Everyone! Stop! Someone will get hurt!" On and on we go with no one giving one inch. A feeling comes through that I must do what I can to protect the smallest and I must do what I can to protect myself. I begin to understand that I will die. Death by popping.

I am amazed throughout at how reasonable I sound to myself. I am, I believe, making perfect sense. What a rational conversation we were having. Surely you must see that these children, your friends, are getting hurt here. Then, as these words emit from my mouth, the first child pops, just like a water balloon. Then the next. And the line shoving up or coming down continues to grow, no matter how many pops occur up front.

Children on the up and down side yell. "Get out of the way! Move!" They insist on gaining the right to pass. An inch of the slide surrendered increases the shoving and the panic. Up-shovers find evil in the down-sliders and

the same is true of the reverse. As my dream lingers, I see no end, no resolution, and nothing I can offer other than preventing a child here or there from popping, mopping up the juice that comes from each popped child, and coming to terms with my own inevitable end.

The dream does not end till I wake. And I wake with no clarity. What was that about?

I am that guy in the middle. I go there under duress and I go there every day. I surrender to a design and a set of outcomes not of my own design. A journey there can commence at any time. I seldom relish being stuck there

Yet, I learn there, in that place where I can't win. The juiciest eye-openers come from the fact that I am stuck in the middle. How could this be true? I learn, kick and scream, in the middle. And though it's not very 'middle' of me to say this: those who have no taste for this journey are on a headlong course toward becoming cranks and shut-ins who have let their worlds shrink. They are missing out on some good stuff.

I feel confident in saying this.

There is nothing wrong with needing to be right. Nothing wrong with wanting my way. I can, on occasion, win and find joy in that fact! I can witness and appreciate the opposite now. But how we talk to one another when we are all getting squished — that's another thing all together. When I yield a little bit, I can expect to move.

How i fight letting go even if it works. We will see how tomorrow unfolds.

Chomp

Carlos and Tamia, both kindergartners, sat on my playground bench this morning. I told them to plant their backsides there until I could clear up a couple of things. Carlos wriggled. His orange sneakers swung back and forth, inches above the ground. Tamia sat calm, hands folded in her lap. Winter sun hung low and bright over the treeless yard.

Perfect time, thought I, to straighten things out:

Carlos, how did those teeth marks get on Tamia's arm?

Tamia held out Exhibit "A" and there, just above her right elbow, I could see a crescent shaped bite mark. No broken skin, but a set of red divots including a snaggle-toothed dent that appeared to match the fang that stuck out in the front of Carlos' upper deck.

I did it on accident.

His brown eyes, two sizes larger than his skull wanted to hold, scanned skyward and made a side-ways cut at the bite mark that Tamia had now shoved close to his face so that he might better recall. His eyes then locked in on mine:

Anything more you want to tell me, Carlos?

Yeah. The part about the monkey. It happens when I hang upside down on the bars. Today, she kept hanging right next to me. She kept bumping me. Then, the monkey came out — the biting kind. I had to bite her. That's what a monkey does.

Can I have some water? Are you gonna call my mom?

I wrote down his words on a form in the box labeled 'assailant's statement'. Other boxes required the students' names, first and last, their numbers, a list of witnesses, a description of the incident, time, date, and a report on the consequence that I might deliver.

So, let me see, Carlos. You turned into a monkey and bit Tamia. Anything else you'd like to say to Tamia?

I'm sorry Tamia.

Tamia held her elbow close to her face to inspect a final time. Then, she looked at him to size him up:

OK, Carlos. This time at least you didn't lie.

With this exchange, both children appeared complete. They hopped off the bench, and darted toward the lunch room.

Equipped with Carlos' monkey story, I considered phone calls I might need to make. Tamia's grandmother had cornered me just two days prior regarding Carlos — 'That little boy messes with my daughter. His mother comes up short. She's a child herself. It's up to you. In my day, we would whoop boys like that one. No questions asked. If you ever want to fill out that jacket you're wearing, you'd do well to pay attention to what I'm saying.'

So, what should I write on my report for today? That I met a boy who could change into a monkey. Should I offer that as a plausible precursor to biting? That he made right by telling the truth? Would that do? The whole scene arrived front-loaded with antecedents and wrapped in circumstances. This stuff wouldn't fly in a write-up.

I get to be between the as-is on the left and the as-desired on the right. So, for today, I refuse to play. Tamia has had her justice delivered in the form of Carlos' honesty. And Carlos got to be a monkey that bites. I am shredding these forms and letting this one stand. I can explain and give it a neat wrap later, if anyone asks.

Gold

On the first day of winter, I remember seeing a small-boned child with a mop of brown-hair. She sat on a broken concrete stoop, cradling head in hands and staring out at a pack of bright-jacketed children dashing in dragon lines up the slide and back down. Tumbling balls of primary colors. This girl made no move to join them. She remained still, alone, in thought.

"Who is that?" "Ariana," the yard teacher told me as she rang the hand bell. "New student?" I asked. "No. She came here last Spring."

As she and her classmates filed in through the big doors. I became more curious.

I walked through the building and made a detour back to her classroom. I entered to find Ariana sitting at a table with four other children. Low sunshine spilled across the room as all of them wrote and drew. All except one, that is.

I made my way to her table:

"Hello." She did not answer. "Are you Ariana?" She looked down. "What did the teacher ask you to do?" No reply. A second child, the one sitting next to her, replied: "She told us write a sentence that tells where we came from. We have to draw a picture too."

"Can you do that?" The girl said nothing. Instead, she sat motionless, a big piece of paper spread out before her. "Go ahead. I'll wait."

Perhaps a full minute passed before she snagged a crayon and scribbled a string of letters. Then, she slammed down her crayon. "Done already? May I read what you wrote?"

Then she spoke his first words to me: "My letters look ugly."

Ariana had written a single sentence, clear enough for me to read. About coming from a house with one daddy and no mommy and about how she got sad sometimes. Intriguing information, but back to the original point — the handwriting was flawless. I could read every letter. I told her so.

"Your printing is perfect. You make beautiful letters."

She sat without speaking. I said, "Can I ask you something? Is there anything else you know you can't do?" The girl looked at me and began to spout a long list — so long that I asked her to stop. "Wait! . . .Let me show you a little trick. What if I knew how to go inside your brain pull out all of the "I can't's? Would you let me try?"

Ariana returned to silence. I saw her glancing, but she wouldn't talk. So, I commenced to wiggle my fingers and tap her forehead. She giggled, and I said "Hold on a second. . . Got it!" and then, I said, "It's out! The biggest 'can't' I ever caught. How do you feel? I'll put it in my coat pocket. OK?"

She nodded. We smiled. I left.

When I passed her in the lunchroom two hours later, she gestured to me: "Can I have the "can't" back." I hesitated, but I let her reach into my inside coat pocket. "I'm gonna throw it away." I watched as she went to the big gray bin to slam the invisible yuck home.

Done!

So, why tell my little tale — this particular moment plucked from a pile of tin? To me, the moment is gold. It provides clues about how to step from under old weight that I never wanted anyway. It offers just enough of a shine to bring a thank you to my lips and a chin-up toward what might come next. For today, I believe that will get me from one end to the other.

Weaving

Three days before it happened, Alex showed me his shark-tooth necklace. One shark tooth, about an inch long, that hung on a string of glass and ceramic beads. He used his thumb like a little paddle to push the tooth closer to my face. Hey look at this! I got this tooth. What do you think?

He folded his arms and made a smug, chin-up face. His friends started poking at him with questions. "Cool. Where the shark tooth came from? How'd you get it? Can I touch it? Sharp!" Alex's round face beamed as he took in the big chief glory.

You can touch it. It's cool.

Three days later, he broke the string when he got to jostling with one of his friends. I think his buddy wanted to grab Alex's chocolate milk — always coveted — and Alex caught the string with his index finger when he bobbled the milk carton. Beads popped off and bounced along concrete. Alex stopped short. His eyes grew. Then he collapsed into a sobbing lump.

His friend Miguel came to tug on my sleeve. Alex! His string came undone. The tooth is gone!

I saw Alex and crouched down low so that he could hear me. He wouldn't look up and he didn't have the strength to stand. Man, I said, we can fix this. We can string the whole thing back together. I promise, I said.

When I used the 'p' word, he lifted his wet and red face, rubbed his hand through his black spiky hair, and made

eye contact — maybe to see whether I meant it. I told him I meant it. Beads had started a slow roll toward the drain. So we got busy.

We got three of his friends together, blocked the drain and worked the concrete deck on our knees. No way to prove it, but I think we found every bead. We also found a set of lost keys that had disappeared an hour before — that's when the next thing happened.

The arc of the weaving grew. We found that the keys belonged to a tall slim man, an uncle of someone who, because he had lost his keys, hadn't been able to go to work. He couldn't start his car without his keys.

When the tall guy got the keys, he said thanks and put a red envelop in my pocket, He told me to give it to the kid. Noting that some kind of cycle was in the works, I gave Alex the envelope. Alex then took the gift in his right hand, passed it to his left, and gave it back to me. You keep it. Thank you.

For Alex, we put his beads and his tooth in a small bag. He said he'd take it to his mom and she would string the necklace again. For the uncle, I didn't have a chance to ask.

Linked wishes, braided hopes, and just the right amount of faith. Even luck. Not stupid luck, but the kind that respects how everything undone comes together in time. Up, over, through. Up, over, through. A good weaver knows to make things come together you need a little bit of muscle and the persistence of the steady pull.

Wisdom

Jordan just turned ten. He is my height. He has a round, soft face, dark brown skin, and a button nose. I have known him for two years and have never seen his face twist in anger nor have I heard him spit out an unkind word.

When my friend, Mr. Charles Tucker from Mississippi, visited Jordan's classroom about a month ago, he met Jordan. Mr. Tucker shared stories about boyhood on the Delta — about how one race treated another at that time, about separate water fountains, sitting in the backs of buses, and strange fruit dangling on hot summer nights. He didn't want to push too hard. Nonetheless, his stories all rolled out fresh as the here and now.

During the subsequent question and answer, Jordan's eye's locked onto Mr. Tucker's. The boy asked his elder "Tell me what makes one man unkind to another? I don't understand what would make anyone want to be mean."

Mr. Tucker looked at me and I tossed it back to him. "The question was directed to you, sir." And Mr. Tucker said, "Son, that is a very thoughtful question. What makes you think to ask a question like that? Thank you, Jordan. Has anyone told you that you may be a philosopher?"

Philosopher. The boy asked for a definition. Mr. Tucker told him that a philosopher was one whose thoughts flowed in the deepest water, coming to the surface only when the time was right.

Jordan beamed the way a child beams when he gets seen.

When we left the room, his teacher whispered to me, "He has never said a word in class. That's the first time I've heard his voice. I don't know what to think."

Since that day a few weeks ago, I, too, have paid closer attention to this ten year-old.

So, yesterday, when Jordan and his friend walked past me on the upper playground, the boy appeared thoughtful. I tugged his sleeve and asked "How you doing, young man? What's on your mind today? Any wisdom you might want to share before the day gets rolling?" He paused, took a breath, gazed up at a pair of clouds circling the yard and said that he would "get back" to me.

"No problem, young man. I can wait."

And with that, he departed, leaning on his friend's shoulder, whispering into the other boy's ear, giggling. Words might come and they might not. Neither he nor I knew when, or from where.

Wisdom is like that, hiding its sources, feigning smallness. However, one can't drop a quarter into a wandering philosopher's skull and expect gold nuggets to roll off the tongue. It rolls as it pleases, slow and steady, a surprise that pops into words, wet, shimmering and churning up from far below the surface. Stunning when at last it comes to light.

Now, my turn to whisper a few questions:

Where do philosophers come from? Ones who can call up shining, essential insights? When the words come, how can one tell truth from fibs? Could this boy be one of those rare ones? Stuck as we are, I look for a day when someone just like this boy might survive to summon bold truths that can shine light on another way.

Might it be you, Jordan? Might you be someone just like that? I'll have to wait to find out.

Waves can roll over everything. They do their work through the slow grind of momentum. They come from the deepest parts of the ocean and travel for days before reaching the shore. A wave can't look back and can't stop until it expends all of its energy. Respect that energy, Principal, or end up floating face down.

Animal

Victor, a first grader, came to school this morning dressed sharp in a bright red shirt, new sneakers and stiff new blue jeans. He bopped more than walked, bounding in rings around his mother who trudged next to him, eyes down on the cracks in the pavement, wearing her weight like a woolen shawl.

The pair came within fifty yards of the playground gate when something in the boy shifted. I heard him growl, saw him claw at the air, and watched him spin to confront unseen critters who approached from above. I could see that his transformation was total. Throughout, however, his mother gave no clue that she noticed anything different.

Onward she trudged

When he and his mother came within feet of the gate, Victor the Wild reverted. He became good little Victor. The change took only a second. Mom murmured good morning and kept walking. So, I spoke to the boy:

How are you?

He grinned. A couple of teeth had yet to fill in. We both watched as his mom ascended the steps to the blacktop without looking back. I took Victor aside for a short walk.. I had to ask a couple of questions:

Who was that who came with you up the hill? Not your mom. I mean the wild guy? Do you know him?

Victor stopped short. What. . Oh. . .That's Wild Man.

Oh, Wild Man. . . I see. . .He seems kind of powerful.

Could you see him?

I could see a lot of him.

Could you see all of him?

I saw a lot. Want to tell me what I missed?

The boy eyed me up and down.

Come on, Victor, I can take it. Tell me about Wild Man. . .

So, he let me have it. About how Wild Man comes on, takes over, scares away the sticky-finger people, makes him strong, tells him to eat raw meat, and lets him "smell everything and hear even the tiny sounds."

Just then, I remembered a piece I had read that spoke of an ancient time - when both people and animals lived in harmony on earth. In that time, a person could become an animal if he wanted to and an animal could become a human being.

Animals and people all spoke the same language. "That was the time when words were like magic. They would suddenly come alive and what people wanted to happen could happen — all you had to do was say it. Nobody could explain this. That's the way it was."

I beheld the boy before me as basketballs flew overhead. Neither of us budged. Instead, he looked me in the eye:

Principal, can I tell you something? Wolf Man is real. He's not pretend. That story is me. Right now. Every day. I can't explain. Do you believe me?

Sometimes magic just shows up. Was this morning one of those times? I came to the edge of a memory both old and shadowed — one that I couldn't quite bring forward. I placed an index finger over my lips. Shhhh! Victor. That's enough for now. Go play! Go!

He split and I puzzled. . .How to make safe the way for this shape-shifting boy?

Might today be a good day to attend to the quiet ones? To the wind bending a single tree or the hawk overhead? Listen both to sounds and silence. Just listen deep and pay attention. Start by saying nothing and breathing. That may be the best place to hear what you have forgotten.

Waking

A climbing structure sits anchored to the north corner of my school's playground. Four thick cords rise from asphalt and come together in a crow's nest twenty feet high. A child with strong hands can scramble up to claim that perch, and from there, she can see west to the shoreline and beyond. Once a child declared to me that, from that nest, she could catch clouds if she had long enough fingers.

Yesterday, a fast moving storm approached from the west. The edge of this storm threw sun-tinged clouds and bursts of rain on shore. As I walked toward the playground, I filled with awe for these clouds — as if they could speak: Here we come! On our way!

I got to the yard's north gate but stopped short. There, overhead, I discovered a child perched in the crow's nest. She faced westward into the wind. Through the gusts, though it was too dark to see detail, I did hear her soft singing. Then, light peeked between the tumble of clouds and I glimpsed the profile of an eleven year old named Dana.

Several puzzling facts required my attention: A young girl, alone at this hour, perched on the crow's nest. While I saw no immediate danger, the girl did seem lost in trance, eyes fixed on a glowing horizon point where sun would soon rise. Clouds piled on and wind kicked up with the smell of rain. Then came a quiet, special thing: Dana's eyes closed, her long hair blew back, and she opened her arms wide like wings. She waited a minute, and then opened her eyes again. Throughout, she had no idea I stood nearby.

A storyteller named Roman Payne once said: "Never did the world make a queen of a girl who hides in houses and dreams without traveling." If I had to guess, I'd say I witnessed a point where at least one child started to take flight!

All these facts speak to a small story: The ragged edge of a fast moving storm. A girl who came to school too early. The absence of parent to accompany her. Then, of course, a solitary, pre-dawn climb upon a piece of playground equipment. My hunch, however, is that the biggest awakenings arrive in pockets like these, when we assume that no one is watching. Words could never suffice to describe what a heart can understand.

Dana opened her eyes and chose to look west. Maybe an angel of solitude descended to sit upon her shoulder. This storm-studded sunrise was hers to hold. I chose to let her be.

"Learning needs no place and change requires no herald."

This quote crossed my mind as I walked into the building and raindrops commenced to fall. I hustled to batten things down and do the reckoning for a rainy school day. Dana, for her part, would soon show up wet, brimming with secrets — coming inside after her encounter with something as big as a storm and as high as thunderheads.

How much I stumble upon when I set out looking for nothing at all!

Rocks

With bangs chopped just above his water-blue eyes, Eric sported a near perfect blond bowl. Beyond this bit of flash, a second fact stood out — that he had conned twenty-two other second graders out of hundreds of dollars. Maybe more. Some weeks ago, I caught a glimpse of his operation.

Rapid movement caught my eye as this boy sat at a round table in the library surrounded by a ring of attentive second graders. I observed for a minute as Eric swept his left hand over the table, tossing out a scattering of bright glass gems. Walla!, said he. Walla! I paused to look, but Eric swept the sparkling show back into a little black bag. Must follow up, I said to myself. I then walked onto the next table.

Fast forward to two weeks later. I sat in my office and became aware that someone was watching me. There stood another tow-head named Luke. Next to him stood his mother. His red eyes told me he had been crying. Mother looked other than pleased.

Luke, tell the principal what happened to your twenty dollars.

Luke pulled out a small nylon pouch. He rattled out the contents — bright glass rocks that sparkled on my table. What are these, I asked. Magic crystals, Luke told me. I bought them from Eric. Mom sneered. Then came the tale of the magic crystals that brought you what you wished for. Still, you had to have all of the colors for the best results. And, the bonus secret spell would cost you five dollars extra. Luke had bought the total package.

After the hang-dog confession, mom demanded that the operation be stopped, spat out a couple of well-I-nevers and stomped out to her next pressing appointment. Luke remained, looking at me, eyes huge as they had been the day I noticed him among other second graders at the table in the library. Luke, I'll see whether I can get your money back, OK?. He stood there, still looking, not budging. You have to promise not to tell my mom this. Yes, Luke? These crystals work. They really are magic. I swear. No. Really! Do you believe me?

He told me how everything had changed since he bought the gems — that the kids in his class now liked him and that they had stopped being mean to him. Then, I followed up, grilling Eric, who, for his part, told me about an old clown-faced guy on the wharf who sold him the glittering rocks. The guy had made sure that Eric knew about their powers. Little guy, said the clown, sometimes you just gotta believe.

Eric shut his business down but I kept an eye on things over the next few days. And, I saw that something had changed — Luke, for example, sat with other children though before he had sat all alone. And more, I heard him telling jokes, and other children laughing at his jokes — not at him. How could this be?

Whenever the traveling salesmen show up on the edge of town, we usher the children inside, whisper time-worn warnings, and hustle to bar the doors. But, when I started this work, I promised not to crush the wide-eyed dreams of children. Everything that is possible resides within these unlikely dreams. A dream, a hope, or a wish — all three of these crack open just-the-facts blindness and let light in.

Yes, Eric — and then Luke — got gamed, but they came away prospecting in the improbable. We can't keep the doors shut all the time. Trick me into growing a bigger heart and a freer mind — I will buy those rocks every time. 53

Tight

On a Monday morning a few weeks ago, I got a nudge from a short, stout fourth grader named Alejandro. He liked to stand next to me on the playground and give me advice. On that morning, he directed my attention to some older girls who were just then arriving:

"Ooo, heads up, Principal. Here come those perfect girls. They tight!"

That which constituted perfection for Alejandro proceeded to arrive. From our center-yard post, we watched as five girls, one by one, showed up in short shorts, little boots, frilly tops and ponytails.

Ella, tall, thin and black-haired, arrived by the west gate. Blue-eyed Eva came from the east. Janetha, light skinned and confident, stepped from the building's back doors along with Allison, the quietest. Sara, roundest, loudest, and least likely of all, arrived last and jammed herself into their gathering ring.

"I didn't see that one coming." I said to my adviser. "Well, there you go." Alejandro replied.

On this particular day, these girls created a blacktop sensation. Even kindergartners paused to comment. When I approached to ask "How you girls doing?" one said, "We good" and added, "Never mind us, principal. We just talking."

Fine by me. Carry on.

One thing pleased me: The ring included Sara. I knew her to be a brawler and a screamer, often at odds with her classmates. Could it be, at last, she had found friends? When we got out toward the third week of clique bliss, my hopes rose. Then, something shifted.

I spotted the group near the water fountain, and saw that five had shrunk to four. The four huddled in a fierce hush and made cutting glances across the yard. And there, Sara stood next to the back gate, hands clenched, looking a a bit like a bomb itching for a spark.

"Oh no. What have we here?" I headed in Sara's direction.

As I got closer, I could hear her cry in a kind of cross between wail and whimper peppered with streaks of cursing such as: "Oooh, that ugly little girl think she cute but she ain't!" and "No one get to talk smack to me like that!" Sara's rants provided no further details.

"Sara?"

"Leave me alone!!"

Whoops. Still too hot. I stepped back to wait, but to no avail. She hadn't cooled down by the recess bell, nor by end of day.

And still today, I saw her standing by herself on the yard, not speaking to anyone. Maybe bleeding a bit on the inside. I had no insight on what had happened and to my outreach, I got a silent no-go.

A fundamental desire is to be a part of something and to belong to someone. Behind any coming together, however, is the coming undone. In comes before out. Climbing begets the tumble down.

I flashed back to Sara that first day when she shoved her way in. She strong-armed a place among these girls and made things work for an instant. Then came the push back and Sara came up short. How often had I seen it go that way?

You'll find your home someday, Sara. No need for principal to be running around, fixing things all the time. Your crying is called for. Best to let it be. For me to remember? That each time through, the teaching and the learning cut a bit deeper.

We grow our souls one hard pass at a time.

Ring

Monday, I find myself in the midst of a rough start that raises questions and casts shadows on the afternoon's prospects. So, I retreat to the kindergarten room where I hope to find peace as the light dims elsewhere. Children are deep in their work so I sit down at one table to join a ring of five year-olds. What time is it? Playtime they say. Perfect, I reply. What a great way to start!

In front of each child is a pile of tiny plastic blocks. A child can attach one block to another and create shapes. I see right away that the only limits might be those residing in the imagination of the builder, but not in the blocks themselves. Given time and the inclination, a child might make a construct of any size and bestow it with any function he chooses.

I sit myself across from a boy who has set out to build airplanes. Waylon. Stern and task-oriented, Waylon trains his gray eyes on the plane he has just about finished. He affixes two more blocks and shifts his attention to what this shape can do. At the last instant, he adds seats to the back, and lets it lift off on a runway only he can see. His plane buzzes over table center and flies up for another round. His big pursed lips provide the buzzing and his wonder-opened eyes fill in the blanks.

The flying plane prompts a response from Adeline, next to Waylon, who then slaps together a wheeled job that she assures me is a truck. Why a truck? I'm going to pick up the people from the plane, she declares, and into the center of the circle goes a second buzzing thing.

Now with plane and truck in motion, petite Jacqueline fills in with an indispensable house — essential for all the people who fly on the plane. She pegs her house together with an arched front door and floor plan that includes a room appended to the back. Who is this room for? For kitty — the kitty that flew in on the plane. She reminds me that every plane must have a kitty on it and every kitty must have a room. Then Armando leans in, shoving together his small pile to make a hammer — a hammer to slam on the plane — he pats the hammer into the palm of his left hand to show that both he and it are ready for duty.

Throughout, I sit next to curly-haired Evangeline who never once touches her pile of blocks. Instead, she watches along with me. We build nothing but ask all the questions. We prompt the stories that link our little ring together. I know that, given time, we both could find a way to add to what the others have started to create.

I am made whole through the watching. I ask the questions, listen for linkages, and learn how individual creation fits in to a larger plan. I hear confidence from each child — that he or she can find a place for himself within this ring and build something that fits in. A child can work himself toward connection, making homes for cats, low-buzzing planes, trucks for people, all brought together through the simple grace of a small circle, where each of us can find a way to make the day we choose.

I knew I came here for a reason. I knew I would not leave disappointed.

55

If I grow quieter, I will hear more. Curiosity will flow into deeper places the way water flows. Who knows? Today is day one. I start by holding my tongue. Holding it even if it pinches. I will keep quiet places safe—and share or celebrate when the time is right.

5.

January

Short Days (Long Nights)

"Wanna see me do a cartwheel?"
"How many times can you go?"
"Lots. I don't know. Here goes.."
"Wait! Wait!"
"What?"
"You might get hurt."
"How about a flip?"
"You can do a flip?"
"Yeah! I can do forward and back."
"How about you don't and just say you did."
"Sure?"
"Yeah, I'm good."

Hand

If a teacher gives even the slightest signal that it's time to go outside, kids hop up and bolt for the door. That's true most of the time. So, this morning, when I got a distress call from Ms. Weathersby telling me that Tarik "is being difficult again. He doesn't want to go out to play" I knew she shared only one part of the story.

I hung up the phone and headed to the classroom tip-toeing through the back door, silent as slipper toes. I watched as twenty children who, at the teacher's signal, scrambled toward the front door. But Tarik, the twenty-first child, remained apart. From the back, I saw his curly black hair. He sat on the table top, hands gripping the table's edge. He kicked a chair, a book shelf, and the table just hard enough to make noise.

The teacher's words — before she noticed me — gave me pause:

"Get your feet off my chair, little boy. Stop kicking my shelves. Don't touch my things." Then, her eyes locked on mine for a rich instant. She spoke again: "He is having a bad day. You handle him. I'm taking my students outside." She exited with entourage in tow.

I determined to address first things first.

I pulled up a tiny chair and sat next to Tarik, asking him what he had been asked to do. He showed me a single page, stuffed with a dozen images of bears, mountains and little people.

"I didn't finish my sentence."

"Can you write it for me now? And can you write your name on it, too?"

He wrote "Puff the Magic Dragon" and asked me how to spell "Dragon." I spelled it out on my hand and he copied. He then signed his name. All of his letters faced the right way! Job well done, from my point of view.

"And your letters are perfect! I'm proud of you." Singular praise, the fact that I gave it, unraveled the knot from his brow. He lifted his head and looked at me.

"I'm gonna sign my paper my own way too" he said as he flipped over the page. He drew a blue outline of his left hand and with a single brown pen filled in the outlined shape in a brown ink, going over it again until it was a deep, shiny brown. His hand print now shone like the color of his skin. He pointed to the hand, looked up at me and said "That's me!"

I got the message. "I am here. My life matters. Teacher, you need to know that."

He sang, dropped his page into the "Done" tray, and took me by the hand to the front door. From there, we saw his classmates forming a circle across the playground. "Playtime now?" I asked as I knelt down next to him. "1, 2, 3, Go!"

Away he went. And though the teacher did not greet him when he arrived at the circle, that snub did not stop him. He nudged his way in at just the point he chose. I am here, I matter, I know you can see me.

Clear, efficient communication. I appreciated that about this boy. How long the odds that the teacher received the message.

I turned to go, considering how the boy had turned his day his way. One hand print, waiting in the "done" box — a message to a grown up to *see* him. For now, his approach addressed the barrier with pure poetry.

Where to begin when we have so far to go.

59

Ear

A sustained barrage of protests came from a pack of first graders who had crammed to one end of their lunch table to bend my ear. I knew that their teacher, Ms. Coolidge, had put a cork in their discourse since August. Now, they had had it. Today was reckoning day and they would have audience for their complaints.

Gabriel, from beneath the chop of his new-cut bangs, sat up to make a statement:

"Principal, You have to listen. Tomas is making problems! I told the yard lady. She didn't do nothing!" (He meant Ms. Henley, a yard monitor with barely a pulse. The boy was probably right. . .)

I stepped back, folded my arms, and said, "OK, go. I'm listening."

Gabriel listed several charges — that Tomas cut him (and everyone) in line all the time, that he had to be first every day, that he always had to win, and so on. The boy tossed in some background information to bring home his case — that even Ms. Warner, the loudest and meanest yard lady of all time, had banned Tomas from playground games. Gabriel announced that she "banned him from the whole universe" as he nodded approval for her actions.

"Tomas and I are supposed to be friends, but today I have to tell on him."

Tomas' eyes welled up as he responded: "I do not cut people all the time. Davida does and she blames me." A grain of rice shot out from between his missing teeth and landed on my lapel. But the hollering did not subside.

Davida, the only girl in the group, retorted with a force that shook her huge pile of curls. "We didn't do nothing! Stop lying Tomas." The story flopped back and forth. Ivan, the only silent child, watched as comments ping-ponged across the table.

I thought to shut the kids down with something like a booming "Silence!" to rumble them into submission. But when I paid attention to the substance of what they said, I noticed the argument was getting somewhere. I let it play out, listening until it hurt. First, Tomas took a bold step and decided to "quit lying" as Davida had suggested. He owned up to his antics.

He then asked his pack a simple question: "What do you want me to do?"

"Just don't be so bossy all the time and let someone else have a turn," said Gabriel.

Tomas said "OK" and the shouting stopped. Not in a gradual way, but in an instant, as if someone had pulled the plug. Sudden silence made such an impact on the lunch room that other kids also became quiet. Damien, a fuzzy headed boy seated at the middle of room summed it up: "Hey, what's going on."

I looked up, recognized my cue, and gave a single direction: "Boys and girls, time to clean up and line up."

"When I am angry I can rave and riot; And when I am spent, I lie quiet as quiet." So says James Reeves in "The Wind" and so, spent, done and speechless, we all began anew. Children closed up their lunch boxes and fell into line. I listened to the ringing in my ears, the music that comes when my lips remain closed.

Time

Tuesday morning, I scooted my way into school just before sunrise and from the start, I got little signals that the day would bring something different. For example, I fumbled in the dark to get my key into the lock on the school's front door. Then, fingers of sunlight extended across the pre-dawn sky and a cool orange glow flooded the doorway. Good morning, I said to no one but myself.

I pulled open the doors, stepped into light spilling from the school's lobby and got a second good morning from a little committee of eight year-olds who had gathered in a card-playing circle on the floor just inside.

"How did you kids get in? Am I the only one who needs a key?"

Not one of them answered. Hmmm. Note-to-self: Must follow up, but not now. Too much to do.

The kids gave a quick smile, and went back to shuffling cards. I stepped over them and dashed toward my office. Not so fast, I heard one child say as she scooped up the deck, and, with the other four, fell in behind me. "We want to see your office!" Oh perfect, I thought. How to start the day when followed by a chatting row of children?

Nosy kids too! We walked in, their questions came in pings:

Is this your office? Where do you keep the money? Can I answer the phones? Where do these (pencils, paperclips, you name it) come from? Can I have one? Please? Who's that in the picture? Oooh she's pretty. Is that your mom? How old are you? Are those your kids? Why do you have all these papers and books? Is this where bad kids sit?

I sat in my chair and tuned out the noise as I sorted a stack of messages from the previous day. However, I noticed that their chatter had stopped. I looked up to see Lillian, smallest but bravest of the five, with her arms folded. She had been studying me.

Yes Lillian, I asked. She examined me again and then spoke: Can I ask you a question? Your face has a lot of wrinkles. Lots of white hairs on your head, too! You even have white hair coming out from your ears! How come?

The other four followed her lead and took to surveying my face, ears, even my knuckles. They paused to inventory each scar and sun spot. Thorough and inquisitive. Still, I felt amused — the focus of an open study, as if they had not, before this moment, taken a good look at the progress of an aging white guy.

These kids were my chorus who, with brown, shining eyes, held up a mirror. I got to see myself reflected back, but felt no shame in what I saw. Still here. Still strong.

We inhabit a life from the inside out. Beginnings require endings to find their balance. When sun poured into my office yesterday morning, I found my heart full of courage for one more day. I took stock in a body that could hold the memory of the whole journey. Then, first recess commenced and the children headed out to play. Onward and free from the weights that older people carry.

That time for carrying a load would come but not quite yet. And for me, now sitting in silence, I breathed in to the chance to witness this cycle of beginnings and endings, taking me down and carrying me over the top once again.

Gate

Rains come this time of year. They wash summer smoke from the air and heal dry cracks in the hillside around the school. As the cracks heal, hill grass shoots up everywhere. Paved patches stand apart from green. Little squares of asphalt-black end in a chain link edge, and the rich black of wet earth begins.

End of school day, Monday afternoon, after the coach ran the kids around the yard a few times, I watched Jake, Jackson, and Matthew — a trio of never-parted third graders who peeled away from their classmates. They walked across the yard and sat, facing outward, shoulder to shoulder by the four-square court near the gate. Each boy chewed his own blade of grass — plucked from where I do not know — and all three sat cross-legged, pulling their boney knees up to their chests.

They had their eyes set on something out beyond the gate. I cast my gaze outward as well. I saw a roll of green grass rippling as the wind whipped uphill toward the playground. Then wind slammed the gate and made the fence posts rattle. "See that?" I heard Matthew say. The other two nodded. See what? I wondered. What are these boys seeing?

I approached them to ask that very question. Oh nothing said they, flashing big toothed grins. A hunch told me these boys wanted out. But they didn't move. Instead they sat in a row of three, still, jaws working, but otherwise silent. Then the bell rang and they lined up for a few seconds. I opened they gate and they flew away.

That a boy subjugates himself to a barrier as trifling as a gate — this fact puzzles me. If you know the inner world of a boy, you know that he wants out. His soul runs in open fields where fall air pours into the lungs like life-giving candy. No hill is too high and every tree invites the climb. Past the fence, his DNA remembers laughing, his legs recall dancing among sounds that bounce when his mates call from the other side. To know it, you have to run with it.

I don't want to participate in the chain of events that amounts that set up traps, and substitutes approximations for living. What would it mean to allow the full articulation of body, mind, and soul? To celebrate the gifts that a good surprise brings? Why the relentless effort to plug energy up, put things down, and fence in freedom? Tether a boy for too long and he forgets how to play. Then you have to work with what happens next.

Da Vinci's diagram of the Vitruvian man, for example, does not depict someone curled, cowering, or ducking as if he were about to be slapped. Instead, he sketches a man who stands in full frontal nakedness, arms extended, and chin up. He looks ahead eye to eye as if to declare I can and I will. I see a sense of confidence in the quest for wholeness, and no hesitation in permitting the unfolding of that which was meant to be.

Whether by straight lines or by curves, let it be. Let us become. That must be what the boys knew but couldn't speak to when they looked out through that locked gate.

Dancing

Last Thursday, several fifth graders and I came together on the upper playground. I had a project in mind and hoped they might help get things started. We stood in a small circle and I put it to them this way:

I want to create something called a labyrinth here. I need your help. Can you work with me?

Sydney, a skinny boy with big glasses, eyed me over the top of his lenses. What do you need? I don't get what you're trying to do.

I knew little more than I could surmise from a printed step-by-step. I read the first step out loud. Sydney then snagged the instructions from my hand. He pulled the paper close to his face, read for two minutes, and lowered the page:

We need to find the middle of the big circle. That comes first. Where should we put the center?

Then, Jacinda, big-haired and full throated sang out — I wanna help. Tell me what to do, Sydney.

Before Sydney could speak, she grabbed a stick of chalk and tossed it to Lucy, a tall, blonde in striped tights. Lucy plucked the hammer and a single nail from my tool bucket, and skipped ten yards away. She put her left foot down: How about here?

Stop! Sydney took my measuring tape and rolled it out to Lucy's foot. He called out two more directions: Make a mark in the middle and one on the outside!

Lucy made two marks and tossed chalk to Travis, a wiry long haired boy who sported a skater sag and white hightops. Sydney spat out numbers and scanned the circle. Diameter of the outside circle, 60 feet! 30 feet from the center marks the outside! Look at the tape! Travis waited for a second, as if computing something. Center circle twelve feet total diameter. Go! Paths, two feet. GO! Tape and chalk began to fly.

Then, Lucy took the tape from Sydney and scrambled in sideways circles around the middle, chalking concentric rings outward, each one wider than the one before. We watched. When she put down the last X on the outer most ring, Sydney wrapped with a short sentence:

Now we are ready to paint!

I called time out! I asked everyone to come back together. Look what you've done! I said and pointed to the blacktop. At our feet, a chalk ghost of a labyrinth now waited. So cool, said Travis. It? felt like dancing! I sent the kids back to class and stayed behind. It came together for me like this:

When finished, the labyrinth will have four chambers. The heart also has four chambers. As I stood on the playground that Thursday, my heart's four chambers opened.

I get these moments where big truths want to rise up. They live in my body, not in my head. Motion and connection bring them out. I tell myself to be quiet — You are getting close. Close, close, ever so close.

Even when you don't know the moves, you can find your way. Ideas can travel without the spoken word. Bodies can dance together, infused by unified visions of beginning and end. I want, more than most things, that young people find ways to open the top hatch and sniff the sweet air of the possible. All awaits, one notch up.

I see myself in the children I work with. When a child gets roughed up by a bully, gets yelled at by a teacher, or watches his parents fight late into the night—all of it gets in. I hope that they (and I) can find resilience to lean in, to stay in, and to have faith. How "unliving" a life makes an endless experience of stepping back.

Stars

When the lights went out during a nighttime performance at the school a few weeks ago, we decided to clear the building and get folks home. Fifteen minutes later, only six neighborhood kids, all in the fourth grade, remained. I told them to gather in the hall under a single emergency light so that we could walk together to their apartment units across the street. Anika, however, had her own idea. She looked up, huge-eyed, to ask me — can we look for some shooting stars first?

Lights-out darkness inside the building met its match when we stepped outside. No city lights as far as we could see. Not even across the bay. Wind must have taken down some major lines. We could see a few red lights on boats in the bay, and car tail lights trailing down streets below. But mostly, it was me, a ring of kids — seven little angels on an impromptu field trip.

We crossed the street to the Open Space and crunched through dry grass toward the middle of the clearing. Wind screamed through the high branches above us. One child stepped on something that snapped and a second child whispered ee-uu-wwah! you just popped a bug brain. That image brought our whole group to a standstill. Wind also stopped and there we stood, in sudden quiet. One by one, taking Anika's advice, we looked up to see stars, blinking, plentiful, everywhere. No one said a word. I looked around me to see open faces, blue-lit by what little light came from above. These were the faces of 'wow'.

I knew these kids. Their moms would not have allowed them outside at night. Not in this city. Not any more.

So, standing under stars as we were was not a common event. Not even for me. More often I look at the ground when I walk at night — and not at the jeweled sky above. Such is my preoccupied habit. And now, here all of us stood, in darkness, witnessing the blessing of this night sky — together.

How do we get as lost as we do? What keeps us looking at the ground, hiding inside, failing to look up even once in a while? Scrapes or scars from old experiences, all of the marks that each encounter leaves behind — and the inclination to sniff sweet smells, soak in deep bands of red that arise at dusk, even stepping out on a night like this one — all of these things get sucked into blackness as though they never existed.

These kinds of shadows can follow us home and wait for us in the morning. They are not the real thing, however. The kids remind me that to see the real thing, I need to look up. Do I take different way home, set aside a few moments for myself, cherish a kindred spirit who remembers how to wonder? What else? That night in the Open Space, Anika tugged on my sleeve and whispered to me: "When I close my eyes I can still see the stars."

What did she mean? I did not understand.

I've thought about her words since that night. Was she onto something bigger — a different way to see beyond just looking? Maybe this: that the best star gazing comes when you reach for them from the inside out. That might be the secret she couldn't quite explain.

Soul

Can we talk about soul? Not about religion or pulpit pounding or efforts by charismatics to snare doubtful explorers for their own ends. Instead, it's about that which wants to rise up to sniff sweet air — to help us remember that we are alive. Maybe it's a nudge that comes in quiet moments, that helps us cradle ourselves through dings and dents. A caress, a subtle re-direct, and soft churning within me. For now, might I let that be what we mean when we say soul?

I had a chat with soul yesterday. It came up as I threw things away, stacks of stuff tagged with notes like — *Urgent, Please respond, Could you please call me* — I had this urge to get underneath the scraps and requests to find more space or maybe a hyphen between tasks completed and others anticipated.

Meanwhile, at the far end of my school's front office, I could see a kindergarten boy hopping and flopping on a little wooden chair like a flapjack on a hot skillet. He had been sent from the classroom where he had been screaming and running over desk tops. My helper told him that he would be going home and that's when the hopping began. He shouted out that he did not want to go home, and did not stop shouting until a driver from social services came to the door to take him.

In the midst of this sequence, I felt something nudging me to notice. But notice what? It was an impulse directing me to pay attention. Was I supposed to hear silence after the little boy left? My own heartbeat, or an almost wordless three words: "You are alive." I hung onto the silence for a bit. I listened to a private exchange within me — one that I did not ruin by allowing interruptions. The social worker stopped to sign the boy out and as she did so he stepped into my doorway. He said, "I see you." And I said, "I see you too". Then the woman scooped him up and they left.

How often do I get pause as I did? I know that because of the demands of my job, I tend to work flat out many days in succession. These days start before sunrise and end when I crawl under the covers late at night. But once in a while, in the midst of paperwork and ringing phones a moment like this one does slip in. I shift to find that I am not the notes on my calendar. My soul, at these times, has a direct shot, an unobstructed path connects me to the children I serve by way of a quiet pathway and brings me into the here and now.

I feel unity in these moments, even with shouting kindergartners. I let myself go there because it's the place where even in profound isolation, I come together. Next step, for me as a leader, and for the kindergarten boy shouting his way out the school's front door is to respect the rules about how souls speak, let them work their magic, and leave all of the talking and explaining to another day.

Joy

I came upon a first grader, Ellery, standing by herself in my school garden. She had on little white shoes and a chiffon dress — both of which made her fit right in with the daisies that popped and bobbed around her feet. But it was her giggling — the pure simple delight of it — that slayed?? me. I decided not to interrupt, but to watch. What in the world did Ellery find to be so funny?

A tall sunflower, as it turns out.

She stood among the daisies, face-to-face with the garden's reigning sunflower — one that towered at twice her height. And, as the sunflower listed and leaned in the breeze, Ellery giggled and chatted away. I couldn't hear a word the flower said, but Ellery understood the entire transmission. Whatever the flower wanted to share with her was just right.

Words I wanted to say? Child, you are adorable! But I held back. Speaking would have snapped the spell and I didn't want to ruin things. I looked to the other side of the garden, saw her teacher beholding the same conversation that I had witnessed. She and I winked and hung back to allow the chat between little person and big flower to conclude of its own accord.

I came home from work and still reminiscing on my little encounter. Then, I took a few moments out front with a Ginkgo tree I planted there a few years ago. A scoop of candy-orange sun still hung in the sky. Earth at my tree's base shone in rich brown and black.

I took some wood chips and spread them at the base of the tree. I watched leaves tumble in the light. I stepped back to take a breath. In the tree itself, I could see early spring buds starting to come forth. I heard the wind, my neighbor's dog, a faint wind chime — no threats, no worries, no sharp edges. Did the light or the leaves have something they wanted me to know?

Simple joy.

Simple joy didn't come in words. It came to me in a warm fullness, a good ache in my bones, and in a keen connection to the coolness of the soil I stood in. My heart, spine, and mind aligned from some rooted place deep underground to a shining angel's hand well above the crown of my head. If any word came to me, it was a 'yes' to right place, right path.

You can't plan for this kind of match between earth, sky and me. And if I see Ellery tomorrow, she may not remember the day before, her little white shoes among the many daisies, and her delighted soul having an earnest chat with something that grown ups would have told her could not speak. Would that she would have many more! Let these delights get counted as real and weighty, just like cloudy days and angry storms.

Celebrate the light dancing as well as its darker cousins. It's not one or the other. Remember, Ellery — and then remind me when I forget — it's both-and! Always both-and. Always all.

I wanted to greet the New Year. I wanted to clear the building of all that had gone down over the past few months. I walked the halls, opened up windows and let the fresh air in. The stale and sour was allowed to escape. It got quite cold but I stayed long enough to allow everything to drain out. Sweet air clears the mind, but it clears the hallways and classrooms too. New questions come on sweet chill breezes. Answers will come when they are ready.

Pinched

A little guy, Michael, entered kindergarten looking harmless enough. It took about an hour to find out that he liked to pinch. In fact, he was a pinching specialist who knew how to pinch with his nails so that he could draw blood. He pinched without warning and didn't let up over time.

He also kicked. Shins, mostly. Grown-up shins made the slower, easier targets. He kicked his classmates, but they sometimes popped him in the mouth, so, by the end of the first month, he stuck to a grown-ups only policy. Big game was best. He took down a social worker assigned to observe him. Single toe-kick below her knee. She requested a revised assignment.

I had to break this situation down in a different way.

What Michael had going for him included speed and a good sense of tactics. I needed to build on these things. My other choice — not a choice really — would include rushing around the building to find the two individuals with the right training to remove him when he next latched onto a teacher, librarian, or my secretary. I didn't want our only recourse to be collaring him and hauling him to a separate room.

When indoor rules fail, time to take the child to the playground. I needed to get to know this boy. I needed to learn his A to B line. What made him smile? What did he want? Why had he learned this pinching and kicking stuff?

I brought a red ball and a curious mind. Michael took my hand without pinching it, and we walked through the double doors onto the big-kid yard. He had not been here before. As we stepped out, he stopped, scanned left to right, and then he ran.

My playground has fences too high even for big kids to climb and during the school day, the gates don't open. I stood and watched as he bolted from one end to the other, climbed half way up a fence, and then came to rest in the middle of a four square court.

I joined him there.

"Let's play give-and-take. I bounce to you and call out 'give.' You catch the ball and call out 'take.' Got it?"

He looked me up and down, stood up, and took a corner on the square. We began.

Basic interaction, reciprocity, confrontation of a healthy kind. These things are more than kid stuff. Grace Lee Boggs, one of my heroes, calls on us to re-imagine how we engage with one another. This boy needed attention, I didn't want to get pinched, but the rule book works only when you know why these rules matter. That's where it seemed I'd have to begin with this boy.

Simple give and take.

I do get scared that I won't find a way. That fear comes up each day. I do get backed into old-school answers to the gaps in the growth of young souls. I need to pause long enough to understand what's going, to map out a plan, and to take on the task of righting imbalances. Or else the pinching and kicking can go on forever.

On the playground with Michael, I found a new way and a first day. May many such days follow on this one and may I find the magical words to keep my colleagues with me as we re-imagine how we engage one another. One day at a time.

Turn

On Tuesday, I had a good feeling about Kennedy. I held one stand-up meeting with my team on the playground. We talked about her progress though she had been a girl who had worked everyone's last nerve. She was coming to school more and fighting less. Progress! Our efforts appeared to be paying off.

We touched on our action plan, went over a couple of back-sliding bits, and sketched out a date for our next blacktop chat. But then, on Wednesday, prior to the final school bell, three individuals in dark suits came to the front office. My secretary called me on the yard telling me they were coming. Kennedy would be removed from school and her home. The dark suited ones came to the yard, picked her up, and they left minutes later.

Just like that. . .

Plans and efforts of five loving individuals came to a standstill. One of us would contact the boy's mother, someone we knew well, to ask how we might help. But we would not pry. Otherwise, she was to become a penciled notation in calendars until we could learn more.

How quickly things turn.

Lots of noise rose up in my head. I wondered whether my efforts (all of our efforts) made a difference. Just that morning, Kennedy had been named team captain for kickball and she had said yes to the assignment. I felt a kind of hole in the middle of my body. Maybe my team felt the same. We had stuck ourselves out on this one.

I need a daily practice that keys in on doing one's personal best as its own kind of reward. Many details do not fall under my jurisdiction, and getting a yank like this can stop a team — and a principal — cold. What practice would help me build stamina to stick it out even when things might change in an instant?

A voice whispered "if you can't love yourself, how you gonna love someone else." Where had I heard that? That's how one shows respect for one's self and the task at hand. If I want to control the result, then I can count on getting 'all tore up.' as one of my colleagues counseled. What are the limits? How can I celebrate what I do control? What in the world might happen tomorrow? And, where had I put that bottle of aspirin?

I was struggling to reconcile my thoughts when, days later, I got a complete answer from watching my kitchen staffer clean the school's stove. Kids had left the lunch line area a disaster, and the refrigerator had broken down. But he approached the task, run on it became an all encompassing mission. The knobs came off, grates came up, and grease pan came out. Only the appropriate cleaners were used.

To me, it appeared that time had stopped or at least that the rest of the world did not matter. If a twister were to rip through the kitchen and lift both him and the stove into the stratosphere, I imagine that he would have been complete until that last moment. This kind of focus was part of what I needed.

Take care of the love in front of your face.

I'm coming to see surrender into the present as key. Maybe there are tricks that I can adopt that will help. But, if I find myself feeling robbed when I confront the unexpected, maybe I need to become the change I wish to see in the world.

I am convinced I'll have ample chances to practice.

6.

February
So Full It Hurts

"Miranda, come on inside the building!"

"No."

"But sweetheart. It's raining."

"I ain't moving."

"Are you going to stand out here all day?"

"Yes."

"But it's warm and safe and dry inside."

"I don't care!"

"I can wait for you right here, sweetie."

"Go away!"

"That's one thing I won't do, my little angel."

"Are you gonna wait there all day?"

"If I have to, honey. Gotta make sure that everything is OK."

Sugar

A first grader named Leonard Taylor caught my eye this morning not so much because of how he moved, but because he did not move at all. That's odd, I thought. Leonard never *stops* moving. Instead, he sat still on his slide-top lookout, bold in his red shirt and big Ben Davis trousers, and motionless. I observed him for a minute, expecting him to slide down. He did not slide.

Judging from the direction of his eyes, I could see he had become hypnotized by the approach of his former kindergarten teacher, Ms. Sanchez, who had entered the playground through the kinder yard gate. The closer she came, the more his little body floated as if in a dream. Then, sixty slow seconds later, there stood Ms. Sanchez looking up from below at her drifty-eyed former student:

"Hello up there Leonard!"
"Hi Ms. Sanchez. Do you remember me?"
"Of course I do, sugar! I could never forget you! You be careful! I don't want to see you fall!"

This visit marked her first return to the site since her retirement last year. Observing their exchange took me in and opened me up to the connection these two must have had the year before. Nothing about this moment should have stood out. But, in witnessing them both, I *felt* that sweet spot that each had set aside for the other.

I had been to Leonard's housing unit across the street several times over the past two years. A house of shouts and tears. Some days, the boy came in so rattled that he couldn't stop shaking. Ms. Sanchez would pile up blankets and a bean bag chair in a place in the corner she called the Big Cozy. The boy could spend an entire school day working from there. No matter how he showed up, she drew him out like a charmer of old, using just the right medicines at just the right time. Quiet cures offered without hesitation.

Some of life's sweetest sugar comes from finding ones we can trust. When a child finds that connection, he will let down his guard. From there, his heart can touch another and in turn be touched. He may remember very few details about time or place. But he will not forget the feeling in these moments. Cradled, seen, safe.

An African proverb tells how, at birth, a child enters the world with his hands closed tight so that he won't lose his gifts. Then, he has to learn to open those hands to release what he has been given. Trust is the secret ingredient in that release.

This boy knew better than to unwrap his fingers for just anybody. He waited for that one who would take him as-is without letting him fall. How lucky to find a teacher with both hands open. How rare to find one who could *see* what the boy kept in his small clenched hands.

When love aligns with opportunity, separation ceases. Opposites merge in realms where eager dreams roll on vast, blue-green fields. A child still dwells in primordial places such as these — sweet spots of black earth — come-together ground that stands sacred, apart from time. Places forsaken by big folk long ago.

Color

I see people in colors. Not skin colors like black or brown or pink though I see these too. Instead, I see their inside colors — a kind of inner glow — or a quality of spirit, an intention, maybe a mood. I can see this kind of color even better with my eyes closed. I do not yet understand what to make of this capacity. But, let these things be for now and suspend your doubt.

Enter young Kenneth whom I stumbled upon midway through my morning rounds a few weeks ago. He had tucked himself behind a big, dented trash can that hot-headed kids often kicked when they got tagged out during kickball games. Most days I did not go as far as that side of the playground. Why this particular day, I do not know.

When I found him, he had little in the way of color — a gloomy gray-green. He had wrapped his thin arms around baggie-jeaned knees. Long blond hair hung over his face leaving only his left eye looking right into mine, green, liquid. His silence in response to my what-are-you-doing-out-here question showed me he didn't want to be found, nor to speak. So, I stood next to him, and whistled a soft Irish tune.

Then his teacher barreled around the corner, planting her heels in the grit and establishing an eye lock with the cringing boy. She spoke — Kenneth, you are a better boy than this. Is this the best choice? Now I know you know what to do. She said all the right words, straight from a teacher's handbook, but her words didn't match her color. Did she mean what she said? Had she quit on this kid already? What was the route of this mismatch?

She turned to go and he stood up, shuffling after her as the clashing duo re-entered the building and ascended the concrete steps. I stood puzzling over what I had just witnessed. The exchange knocked me back to my grade school years, where the boy in me stood at the feet of his teacher, confused, hearing the soft twisted warble of a twisted logic that cut rather than clarified.

When I came to, I resumed my rounds along the edge of the yard. What came to me was a simple truth — that blue on the outside becomes the blue within. We are permeable. The reverse is also true. I may see these truths as colors, but everyone sees truth in some form or another as it conveys itself from the deep inside of one to the hidden heart of another.

Some day, I will find faith in self. I'll see pearls laying in wait, ready for the beholding. I won't look backward asking what I should have said or should have done. In such a yet-to-be moment, thought and act will splash my sky in one rich stroke — painting a bright stripe that requires less talk and much more walk.

Box

At times, the hilltop itself speaks to me. Monday morning, for example, when I walked through the school's front archway before sunrise, I spotted an epigram engraved into the stone above: ***"Education is bitter but the fruit is sweet."*** How had I missed it? The engraving had to be as old as the building itself. Then, a chill wind whipped and shoved me just inside the doorway. There, I paused a second time.

"Hmmm. I'm listening." I said to the brick walls and the worn tile floor.

I approached the center stairway and paused once more. A loud male voice rose from downstairs. I made rapid descent, and whooshed into the first floor hallway. Lights out, still dark. I moved on, pushing open two back doors that exited the building. There, on the wet asphalt of an empty play yard, I found a child, Raymond, and his father, Lucas. Father towered over son. A tense exchange appeared imminent:

I heard these shouted words: "What the hell were you doing? You got no brains, boy? Can't you just think for once?" I saw father raise index and middle finger. He took aim as if to make blunt impact on the boy's forehead. I moved to intervene:

"Gentlemen, how might I help you this morning?"

When father heard me, he froze and dropped his hands to his side. The two stood still, boy looking down, and father looking away. Lucas left the yard, and Raymond watched him go as pre-dawn wind blew back the boy's big head of curly hair. Raymond shoved his hands in his jeans pockets, shivering in his big flannel shirt.

"Come on in 'til the bell rings. Too early to be out here, Raymond."

I held the door for him as we both went inside. As we climbed the stairs, I saw that he wore no socks and his sneakers had holes in the heels. "Anything you want to tell me, son?" asked I, just once. I hoped that he might speak to me. He, however, remained silent as we turned from stairway into the bright office fluorescents.

I could find no rules that Raymond adhered to, no guidelines that helped me to direct him, and no vessel able to contain the energy he brought. On a given day, he might sing in the midst of an exam, decide to put ketchup down the back of Carmen's pants, lick Edgar's face, or jump from table to table in the lunch room. No matter the shape of the box, he had way of breaking free from that which bound him.

Yes, father yelled at his boy and raised his hand. I, too, fell to a short list of blunt words in my attempts to break through. Raymond continued to run wild, regardless. To borrow from a poet named David Whyte, his life appeared driven by momentum against which we have no defense.

I watched and wished for guidance to help him find footing when the right time came. No stigmas and no judgment. Instead, I thought about the goats that used to roam this hilltop and the fruit trees that once grew here. Might it be that sweet fruit can arise from a day that starts this way? Not only the bitter and hard-pitted plums? And might that sweeter fruit need nothing more than time and patience to ripen, nurtured by a gentler hand?

Just these thoughts I took with me as sunrise chased away night, and boy and I made room for another day.

Surrender is key. Nothing weak about it. If I let something go, I can be more present. I can better prepare for surprises. Maybe bigger, more poignant truths can come through when I have let go. What is the tactic here? How do I do this? What is the first step?

Tattoo

Matthew, a fast sneakered ten-year old, beat me to the playground this morning. Better to say he bolted across the blacktop. I didn't try to keep up. He jumped on the monkey bars, and grasped the high bar with his left hand. With blond hair, wiry frame wriggling in a Captain America t-shirt, and near-shredded blue jeans, Matthew came wrapped in a raw uniform to match his untempered spirit. Recess had begun.

As he swung, he waved with his free hand. "Hey Principal!" His clear, high voice floated across the yard. I headed his direction and heard his voice again, "Where is everybody?"

Good question! I checked my watch. No other classes had come out. Just the two of us so far. "Not sure what's up. Where's your class, by the way?" He pointed toward the back steps. A few children started to spill out. However, as he pointed, I noticed a fresh string of kid tattoos on his left forearm — as many as seven small images extending from elbow to wrist.

"Hey Matthew, tell me about those tattoos on your arm." He dropped to the mat, came over to me, and raised his arm out in front of his body.

"Will they wash off?"
"These are my whole story."
He pointed to the lightening bolt.
"This one is the beginning."
"The beginning?"

"It starts here!"
"But why a lightening bolt?"

Matthew stepped in front of me.

"Do you have to ask?"
"Oh, I see. You are the bolt itself. So what about the two fish."

He began to deliver a proclamation as he described the second tattoo. Both of us walked to the center of the playground. Balls hurtled overhead, jump ropes slapped the asphalt, but I missed all of it. Matthew had me hooked, tattoo by tattoo, from elbow to wrist. Here's what the pictures told me:

Two fish swim around a spot in the ocean — the precise spot where a lightning bolt struck. From there, a cloud of three wishes floats up. The same cloud appears again in the fourth inking, and sprinkles rains onto a single flower. The flower unfolds into a bright star.

"That star stands for who I am right now."

The sixth image is of two eyes. "Eyes that can see everywhere. They look around to make sure everything is cool." And last he pointed out the biggest tattoo of the set — a shining sun, with orange and purple rays stretching out in all directions.

"My stepdad told me that one day I'll shine like this sun. That's why I put it last."
"Is that the end?"
"Yeah. What do you think?" I scanned the images wondering how he came up with this story. But I would have to wait to ask further questions. He took off to join his friends on the kickball diamond.
"Oh, hey! See you later!"

OK. So what? How about this: That when any one of us wanders into a dark corner, we can use the torch of a well spun story to chase shadows away. Talk it up and tell it tall. And also this: That I am no different from this boy. Let me spin myths and repeat myself until I have my speech down pat. With practice, it's the story itself that lifts me up and helps me find my way back home.

77

Crow

When I came in to the front entrance to the school this morning I saw a squad car parked there. Hmmm, I puzzled. School is closed today. What's up?

I parked and approached to find an officer engaged in loud conversation with two women, both of whom cried and made big gestures with their hands and arms. Then, I saw one of my students, Gabriel, seated on the curb out front, with his little cap pulled low over the eyes, coat zipped to the top, and brand new sneakers tapping a puddle of run-off water at his feet. He watched as the officer and the two women talked. When the boy saw me, he made a tiny wave.

What's going on, Gabriel?

Just the facts: Mom (now chatting with officer) dropped him off at 8 AM. She left. He tried to get in, found the door locked, and returned to the curb. Time now: 12 Noon. Events that transpired between 8:00 and Noon, thus far, unknown. Any of us might fill in the blanks with our best guesses. Both mom and aunt were now on scene.

So, I sat next to him on the curb. We didn't talk for a few minutes. I scanned the street to the east and the west. On the guard rail in front of Hilltop Market, three guys stood and watched. Down the hill the other way, parked cars, an empty street, and the freeway roaring by. One guy across the street slept on a bench. Quite a cast.

I asked Gabriel, what have you been doing all this time?

He clapped his hands twice, looked up at me, then to his mom who continued to cry and chat with the officer.

Those two seemed to be hitting it off. So Gabriel turned his chilled nose my way again.

I watched cars and waited. A lady came to talk to me and ask me for money. I gave her a dollar. Then she left and I talked to some birds. Those big ones up there.

He pointed to the wire overhead. Five shiny black crows sat above both of us, beaks turned. They can see us, the boy explained, but they have to look with one eye.

Gabriel closed his right eye, angled his head a quarter turn clockwise, and gave me the one-eyed crow look.

What happens next after a morning like this? I had nothing to compare his experience to in my life. . .getting dumped on a curbside. I know that five year-olds are pure potential. Some kids go places and others crash early. Some get everything and make nothing of it. But how can others build great things from next-to-nothing?

I have heard the many stories: of the man who sat beneath a tree for forty-nine days, returning from his dreaming to a full moon and the power to see things as they are. Or the man who disappeared for thirty years to return curing the sick and raising the dead. Or the guy who got knocked from his horse by a bolt of lightning and woke up talking to angels? Or even Saint Francis who talked to birds all the time.

Then comes Gabriel who sat for hours on this gritted curb and now talks to crows. What did they tell him? At this moment, as his mom chats and crows watch, something has shifted. My wish for the boy: may that which is unforgettable prove beneficial in the end.

Backward

Children walk to school by one of two roads. Each road rises from the flats and ends at the school's gates. The road that rises from the Bay side we call the back way. A couple of days ago, I drove to school, taking the back way, and as I zipped up the hill, I noticed a girl sporting over-sized sweat pants and blonde dreads. She was walking backward downhill.

I slowed, stopped, then reversed. In a second, I had pulled side by side. The hair hung forward over her face, but I recognized her as a fifth grader in Ms. Craig's class.

Emily?

She didn't respond so I pulled over, hopped out and approached. Green eyes looked up, welled up, and looked down. She resumed her backward descent. I started walking backward with her, hoping a clue about next steps might descend from above.

The playground gate stood open about fifty yards up hill. I looked back over my shoulder to see where we might be heading. I could see the back door to her aunt's apartment, opened, but dark.

We walked without talking for half a minute. Then, I spoke up. Emily, can you fill me in? Where are we going?

The girl stopped and so did I. We both stood underneath a big oak tree — the only tree that remained along the side of the back way. I didn't look at my watch, but I felt minutes slipping by. Emily then pulled a smudged and folded piece of card stock from her small t-shirt pocket. On top of the folded page, in Emily's uneven cursive: Backward Spell.

She explained:

"We have to move. My aunt can't find a new job and they want to move us by the end of next week. This spell is supposed to turn things around. Now, since I'm talking to you, I think I have to start from the top again."

"Great. I happen to be going that way. Maybe, while we walk, you can tell me whatever else you want me to know."

Words spilled out about the many broken things, how they got broken, how she and her aunt and her little brother had tried plan after plan. I shared with her what I knew about reaching out, missing, doubting, and searching to find my way by many different paths. Sometimes, even right things seem wrong. You find yourself retreating before you've taken a first step.

We can't make change happen that way. You have to keep moving.

We walked through the gate and onto the playground. With morning recess in mid-flight, red balls flew and jump ropes slapped wet blacktop. We wound our way through games and good mornings. I said to her "let me see what I can do."

She stepped into a four square game and I vanished through the double doors. I had wanted to tell her more — that we can go only forward. Backward, dear Emily, is a way of hiding the fact that we keep moving. Dreams vanish in the smoke of magic charms. The unanticipated — the inexplicable — arrives on its own terms and gives us just enough to carry us over.

To her and with my inside voice, I made this promise: You're worth the time, kid. I'll do the best I can.

Chalk

On Tuesday, chalk came out for recess. On Wednesday the blacktop exploded in powdered gridlines of blue, orange, and yellow. Sketches everywhere charted the mental scatter-shot of eight year-olds — hundreds of secrets written in block-letter code, boy-loves-girl scandals shared in head-to-head whisper rings, now out for public viewing. Our playground had become a 100 square-foot tell-all.

As with every week, chalk day begins with thunder-two hundred feet rumbling down concrete stairs. Chalk buckets — two of them, wait on each side of the big door to the yard. Small fists punch into the chalk as children run past. They then run to the far side of the playground and commence to draw.

This particular Wednesday, when a doubtful sky threatened rain, I stepped onto the yard to walk through sketches kids had left behind. I found dozens of word chains — "Raymond has a nasty" and "I love my mommy". . ."Daddy Macky" written in orange and blue fifteen times. Also I saw box houses drawn with too-big windows, crooked doors and the ever-shining chalk suns.

Also, I found dozens of huge-headed, grinning stick figures, jumping, looking happy. I got hooked by one recurring image — a stick-boy with a starfish head, holding his three-fingered hands up, one hand clutching something sharp — maybe a knife. He also had an open mouth full of pointed triangles for teeth. The same image appeared six times, the boy standing alone in every instance.

I had taken in just a bit of this transient masterpiece when I felt a raindrop. Then another. I stood my ground for a minute. Chalk darkened from moisture. My quiet reverie ceased when I became aware that I was no longer alone. Kimberly, age nine, had tip-toed onto the playground and now stood to my right.

What are you doing out here, Principal? It's raining. Then, I asked "Kimberly, how long have you been standing here?" "A long time, she said." Our talking ceased and we looked at the playground together. It didn't take long before stick figures started to blur.

All gone? She asked. Soon, I answered. Soon.

I brought Kimberly indoors. We walked from the playground in silence. Her red and blue sneakers and my rubber-soled shoes rendered our walk a soundless one. When we got upstairs, I asked her to wait in the chair outside my office. Most kids wouldn't be arriving to school for another half hour.

I closed my door and stopped moving for a second. I wanted to complete my thoughts about the way the playground must hold hundreds of stories — records that we walk on, sweep aside, wash down. Even as dust, stick-boys have resilient spirits that tuck into pores and cracks in the gravel. They may fade, but a faint essence remains, year after year.

Could that be true?

Fifteen minutes passed. I looked out the window to see that the rain had stopped. Sun popped out. Then, children showed up in fives and tens. Time for yard duty so Kimberly and I went outside to the damp yard. Sweet air floated in a post-rain breeze. 8:40AM brought line up time. Kimberly walked to the end of her third grade line and in through the doors they went.

I looked across the yard. Nothing but a big puddle. All gone Kimberly? My hunch is that there is no such thing as all gone. I watched the kids go into the building. For a minute, I stayed among the little chalk ghosts — all friendly, all real. All here holding me up to face a new learning day.

Erased

This morning, I stood on the edge of the playground, watching kids interact. Recess flowed and children's voices wafted in ways that gave me an inkling of a harmony arising from the middle of the earth. Seamless alignment between above and below.

Then, a colleague of mine named Jacqueline, a principal from a school down the hill showed up. She waved as she came through the gate and crossed the yard. Glad to see her, but this couldn't be good news.

"Sister J? What brings you here?"
"I'm in a spot, principal. You got a minute?"
"For you, I'm all ears."

And with that, she unfurled a doozy — how she had stood in a classroom two hours earlier, observing a teacher named Ms. Jennings, who, in her view, was "on something." This teacher stood at the front of her classroom as paper airplanes flew, children wrestled, and most had their backs turned away.

Then, through the noise and flying objects, Principal Jacqueline spotted Felipe, a black-haired eight year-old who shuffled army-style along the carpeted floor. She and this child went way back as this principal had intervened in his playground scuffles a half dozen times. This wiry eight year-old, on this day, had a mission.

Blue jeans sagging and elbows dragging, he crawled closer to his teacher, one tug at a time. Pull, pull, pause. Wait, watch, repeat. One final tug brought him to her feet, but because of where and how she stood behind her big table, Ms. Jennings could not see him there. My colleague leaned forward as if to intevene, but the next sequence moved too fast. The boy pulled a big pencil from his back pocket, rubbed the eraser on the carpet to create heat with friction, and them bam! He stuck the hot eraser into the puffy flesh on the top of her foot.

Of course she screamed — a burst of sound cut through and brought the chaotic classroom to a silent stop. "Get him out of here!" was the only complete sentence Ms. Jennings managed to form.

Jacqueline did contact Felipe's parents, met with the father on the playground, spoke to him about what had happened, and watched as the two left the yard. The part that she did not share was Felipe's answer to this principal's question: Why did you put the hot eraser on your teacher's foot?

"Because I wanted to burn her." But why did you want to burn your teacher? "Because I wanted to see if she was alive."

So, Jacqueline came to my playground because she could find no solace on hers. How could things have come to this point? How could a child have questioned something so basic? I suggested to her that the ability to stand up did not equate to proof of living.

"A teacher has to bring more than that." I said.

I didn't know this kid, but I found myself asking what I always ask. How do we find ourselves sometimes so far apart? What makes a child or a grown up drop back from the pack as both teacher and child had done?

My colleague guessed that today would be Ms. Jennings' last as a result of this boy's action. I guessed that Felipe's journey, for the near term, might continue as a shift between extremes — hard left then a sharp right — zig zagging down pathways where, even with an eraser's smudge, a child can get wiped out by nothing more profound than his second to last mistake.

How do I do this? What is the first step? Help me by standing where I am standing. Stand with me to work among the riddles that keep on coming. Sing in my key, dance in my shoes, and mix it up with me. At least come half way. Call me out. Push me when I need it. Challenge me to help me grow. Make me be my better-than-best. But walk my walk before you tell me what to do. And don't you dare look for the quick way out.

Mouse

A mouse is a great equalizer. Need more explanation? How about this:

Angela, fireplug of a 5th grade girl, stood atop my school's beat-up play structure this afternoon the way she does every day, fists on hips, jaw set. The Crusher as the kids called her. An old school bully. She lorded over more than that old structure. She topped the whole playground. Not one recorded instance of a time where she backed down. She did not say much. She did not need to.

Today, when she took her recess position, she smacked her gums, waited, watched and paid no mind as the sounds of students' singing voices floated down from the third floor.

The playground took on a high noon feeling and I didn't like it one bit.

I had known tough nuts like Angela. Different decades, different hairstyles, same delivery. She divided the playground into those who "messed" with her and those who did not. She found a new target every day and she looked for ways to take that target out. Today, she was looking for Ronnie.

"That boy getting on my nerves" was Ronny's main offence.

He had peed his pants at first recess as students waited in line. She had stood behind him and when he had his moment, she called out "eeeuuuuwah" loud enough for all to turn. Teacher sent the rest of the class inside, and sent Ronnie to the office for a change.

I saw Angela looking back as she entered the building. I could see her lips form a dozen or so words, could see her nod and stop speaking and then step through the doorway. As she marked Ronnie, what was Ronnie thinking? Maybe phrases like "why she looking at me — no one gonna help me — I am lost."

Noon recess was to be her chance to call him out once more.

Turns like these are true crushers. They have happened on playgrounds as long as playgrounds have existed. Angela was no more than today's functionary. Ronnie avoided her by staying in the lunchroom until the bell rang. I decided to follow their class indoors after the bell.

That's when the law of cause and effect struck.

Kids sat reading. I pulled a book from the shelf, found a desk near the back, and read along with them. The room got quiet. Then came a scurry, a scuffle, and a scream. A mouse, maybe two inches long, popped from within Angela's desk. It shot out, ran up her arm, and jumped to the chalk tray next to her. She collapsed and a commotion ensued. Ronnie sat behind Angela and watched the whole thing.

Angela fell to the floor and lay there for a good minute before anyone paused to help. My guess is that her classmates found her high pitched scream as much of a shock as a mouse. Undone, stripped in front of pointing and laughing.

"Did y'all see Angela? She almost died and that mouse weighed a ounce and a half."

The teacher slammed her big book shut and the class fell silent. I nodded, grinned, and stepped out the back door.

Was I mistaken, or did I see a smile on Ronnie's face?

Toughness is pretence. Good shell, but empty in the end. Even with clenched jaw, it all gets in. Trust that life, like mice, is an equalizer. Remain alert. It may not appear so at first, but all will work out in time.

Justice

On the playground, efficiency justice sometimes prevails. Hit me, I hit you back. And don't be fooled by the tears. The picked-on kid cries not only because he gets hurt, but also because he hasn't figured out his next move.

Grown-ups survive beyond the playground because they modify this direct approach. They either up the game and bring in bigger guns, or they change the game and embrace influence over force.

I was in the weeds on this question of justice this week. My goal was always to bring about fairness, but also to plant seeds for a deeper take on what fairness means.

For example, a fourth grade boy snuck into his classroom during recess and destroyed every student's California Mission project by smashing them, pouring milk on them or whatever other opportunity presented. Would it surprise anyone to see the teacher, moments later, dragging that student by the arm to my office? And what kind of justice might this teacher want? What motivated his act and how could he restore balance?

On this day came a kindergartner skilled at spitting. She managed to spit into another little girl's mouth from five feet away. What might you imagine the victim's father had to say when he came to my office? I protected the spitter's identity and said that she wasn't in school that day. The father said he'd be back.

On or off the playground, where does the balance come? And when they demand an eye for an eye — grownups mean for other people's kids. They wrapped their rage in phrases like "You need to send a message." Or "Teach him a lesson he'll never forget."

Revenge isn't the way and please don't get confused about the difference between revenge and restoration. Call all things by their rightful names. And, if we want to offer a restorative path, how would you name the right steps? What happens when the injury to body or soul is a severe one? Please don't talk to me about discipline and teaching if your form of teaching includes adding yet another injury. For example:

Today, I called in a boy, a girl, and their parents. He had pushed her off of the high bar and she had landed so as to break her arm. I asked the boy to make a written and a spoken apology to the girl, to her mother, and her father. I left it to the father of the injured girl to forgive or not.

A risk, but it worked. The arm is in a cast, but justice will help the healing.

Such thoughts as these are running through my mind as I look out my office door to see a fifth grader who was sent to me for the tenth time because he calls a classmate a "fatso." I want him to hurt as she has for what he has done. He may feel nothing.

Justice, unlike vengeance, is not swift. It requires reflection about the causes that lead to a harmful act. It required reflection about intention. And, it requires an eye to the long game. If take this step now, how will that shift my direction in the weeks and months ahead.

Right work. Healing work. Not to call time before we have done. That must be the way forward.

7.

March

Grit Makes Gold

"You've been trying to drop that basketball through the hoop for ten minutes."

"My daddy told me to close my eyes, picture the hoop, and let it fly."

"You mean you're taking shots with your eyes closed?"

"Yes sir."

"Are you sure?"

"He said, you just gotta trust that one thing hooks to the other.

"OK. Sounds deep."

"I don't know how this works. I just know that it does."

"So what are you going to do?"

"Keep tryin'."

"Away you go."

Earth

I may never know how it feels to fly in a rocket or to hover above the Earth. I will not know the gift of flight, taking off like a hawk, nor behold from such a height the painted squares that divide playgrounds.

But after school today, I did at least walk up the hill with three amazing young people. We walked along a dirt trail toward Hawk's Rock — the highest point above the school. Evangeline, Myra, and Grace went ahead of me since they knew the way well. The Rock sat like a watchful elder, half way between the school and houses on the other side of the hill. When I went there, I went to watch hawks fly, see cars zip by and kiss the sea breeze from the west.

I caught up with the girls. They faced south looking all the way to where the curving planet disappeared at the horizon. Today's view had cobalt clarity. They didn't say they minded letting me stand along side and share this vista with them.

I got a chill from my toes to the crown of my head. The planet had a few things to tell me. With the girls, I scanned the horizon for a minute. Then, Evangeline, curly hair parted and tied in two wings, lifted her chin to make a short declaration. "Earth is a big, flying rock." Her two friends giggled but added no further comments. So I asked a follow up question.

"Really? How does it feel? To stand on a flying rock?"

She explained how the rock flies through space, how other planets fly as well, and how very tiny she felt standing here on this day. When she finished, she paused and then signaled her friends to come along. They said "bye" and homeward they went. I stayed on to take in the all-in-all on this cloudless day.

I got to considering my predicament as a human being, destined to live out my days on a flying rock. How often I wished to be some type of animal other than a human — to fly, to shape-shift, to travel through time. Maybe humans are unique in yearning to be other than they are. And still, for all the wishing, we remain thin skinned, mid-sized animals. Only the very few will ever move beyond our planet's gravitational pull.

A 10,000 foot view offers plenty. Seeing what a cloud sees as it floats over our scrambling could save us from countless missteps. However, if you get too hooked on the sky, you forget about the wisdom that comes from having two feet nestled in the rich soft dirt. Everything grows from the ground up — at least everything that matters to me.

My school and my life — the lives of every child that flies along side me on this rock — change in each moment. Evangeline called it out as she stood here. I can't fly, but I have — we have — learned ways to make a go at what we've been given.

Leave the big picture to clouds. Give it to me, the hand to hand, moment to moment. Intuition, receptivity, steadiness, and flow. These come to us at the ground level. May we invite the direct contact. May we feel it sink in. Let all the airborne mysteries have their heavenly place. I know that I am where I belong, here, among the rocks, the grit and the grass.

Right here on earth.

Courage coupled with calm — a pairing that escapes me at times. Even as a boy, I became doubtful, paused, weighed choices, and second-guessed everything. My mother tells me I never sat on any chair without looking at it first. The confidence to act has had to work its way up. I can't keep waiting for a sign. These are the times when we must make signs of our own.

Vavoom!

I got in the middle of a situation this morning that involved a tiny and hooded fifth grade girl. Her proper name was Arianna, but I took to calling her Vavoom five years ago when I first heard her voice. She reminded me of an old-time cartoon character — Vavoom — who could blow holes through mountains with one yell. My Vavoom had a voice like that and because she could be loud, she got the last word often enough.

Before school, I saw her facing off with another neighborhood girl who stood outside the playground fence. Vavoom got heated and delivered her signature sound blast. Ayesha, her foe, backed up several paces. Both girls came away with diamond-shaped rust imprints on their faces from pressing against the chain link. That's how in-your-face this encounter had become.

I knew Ayesha some. Tough kid who had no fear of fighting for her causes. Once challenged, she would come back — with friends — to even things up. As she turned to go, I considered prospects: Would she gather a crew and arrange a "business meeting" on the back end of the day?

Meanwhile, I checked in with Vavoom. She admitted right away that she stirred up this mess. She confessed that she wanted to clean things up. With only a handful of pertinent details, I arranged a face-to-face between her and Ayesha. We would go to the other girl's school and nip things before they got ugly. I hoped to have this one in the bag to prevent a blow back.

Before we had walked three blocks, however, I got a call from the other school. Had I seen Ayesha? She had walked on campus and then departed. The principal there had called the girl's home. No luck. My whole gut tightened. Now what?

We turned around and started back. Then, two blocks from school, Vavoom pulled up short. Ayesha and her two big sisters stepped onto the sidewalk, blocking our way. I made as if to stand between the two sides, but Ayesha's sisters asked me to stand down. "We've got this."

I stepped aside.

Ayesha spoke. She was tired of fighting. Tired of yelling. Fed up with all of it. Vavoom said the same. They went back and forth with a succession of blunt statements redefining boundaries and re-setting rules of engagement. "We stick to that and we done. Here and now."

Just like that! Clean, clear, and complete. And, in that moment, I hardly recognized Vavoom.

After the girls parted. Vavoom and I began walking back. Then, she stopped to make a request:

"In a month, I'm gone from this school. You been calling me Vavoom all these years. But could you start calling me Arianna? That's my real name."

How fast the loud and feisty fighter grew up. A little ten year old stating her needs? Right there, big soul rise up inside a tiny body to be seen and counted.

Days quicken when you reach my age. Blink and you miss big stuff. Likewise, change comes quick and cuts deep. I said not one more word as we walked up the back steps through the school doors, watched over by kindly sunshine, blessed by a single cloud as it drifted out and away.

89

Pink

Viviana cries every day. This morning she came to me with wet cheeks. I knew that once sobbing started, she could continue for a long while.

"What is the matter sweetheart?"

Between sobs and sucking in air, she told me that Alvin, a square-jawed, pebble—eyed, unsmiling brick of a fourth grader, had called her a cry baby. A stupid little crybaby to be precise. And he repeated the words — stupid crybaby — several times, as if to make it so.

Hard-edged stuff that spilled from her classmates' mouths when Viviana could not handle it. Never had I met a child as thin skinned. Today, in her blue tights and red high-tops, this third grader made an easy mark — tossed into battle with no defenses whatsoever.

All of these circumstances came to a head as she took in air for another big wail. I wished I could find a way to make her stop. Instead, I fanned her face with my clipboard as if to cool the pink flush in her cheeks.

Don't cry . . stop, stop . . .breathe . . talk to me. . . tell me what happened. .

No use. Tears rolled up and over, flooding out, punctuated by repeated claims of injustice. What I hadn't noticed was Alvin, her adversary standing a few feet away, arms crossed, eyes rolling. Then he cut in:

"Shut up Viviana. You cry all the time. Big crybaby."

Now Viviana went up another notch. No turning back. Viviana cried with abandon. She seemed to rise up and sink under at least five times. She dissolved and melted down into a little heap. A small cluster of children and I gathered around her and waited. I stepped in front of her, studied her face and tried to find some little inkling of how to help.

It came to me that this little girl was made of water. Sounds, scents, even thoughts poured in. Alvin was the opposite; a little rock with not a hint of emotion. Not a bad kid. But not the kind of boy who might understand that his words could pack a punch. In that moment I wished I could draw on my own element — the power of air- to blow away this stand off. Viviana, a little puddle, spilled out everywhere. Alvin stood his ground, staring at her. A classmate had to shove him back to get him to move.

Then, the bell rang and the exchange ended. As if on cue, the girl sucked in her sobbs, wiped her face, stood up and joined her class' line. Alvin dropped his arms and eased a bit and got in a last word:

"That girl keep wasting my time!" And that was that. Game over.

I stood by myself where we all had been. Great problem solver, Grand reckoner. What a difference I had not made — strong as a wish. A will o' the wisp blowing in, assertive as a question. Not the kind of air power I had wished for.

I coached myself as I left the yard. Ease up. Change comes no matter what. Maybe because of you or maybe not. You may never get to know. Persistence, Principal. That has to be both the target and your take away at the end.

Matches

Big surprises can arrive in quiet ways. That's how I met my newest fire-starter, Xavier. Ms. Carter brought the curly-haired, big spectacled second grader through my door. Young boy and older woman stood just inside the doorway, waiting for me to look up.

"Excuse me, Principal." Ms. Carter began. "I found Xavier behind the bungalows, with these." She reached into her bag and pulled out a box of Ohio Blue Tip matches. Ah yes. I remembered them well. She then pulled out a small pile of kindling — random bits of a torn-up crayon drawing, a shredded spelling test, and some leaves.

Ms. Carter laid out more than sixty matches, spent and blackened. She told me she had found Xavier doing what he could to start a fire. The boy looked at Ms. Carter - stout as a fact. He then looked at me. Ms. Carter stepped out and it became my turn to ask some questions. I had just the beginning of what I might need to know.

First came lies. The standard set: I didn't do it. My sister stuck the matches in my backpack. I don't know how they got lit. After a minute squandered in this way, we managed to back-and-forth our way to a version of truth that we both could live with. He had tried to start a fire in the alley behind the building. He knew the building to be made of dry wood. "Old and dry." He clarified. A stiff breeze had snuffed his matches at least sixty times.

"Do you have anything else you want to tell me?" I asked him. "No, I'm good." Then we both became quiet.

When I was eight, I played with fire, just like Xavier. I didn't want to burn things down or make a big scene. I just remember becoming fused with the energy that arises from the act itself. Something primal lives in fire.

Fast forward to now to a context where boys can't roam, where initiation rituals show up as prohibitions and misdemeanors, and I ask myself how boys sort through the right use of power. With no place to practice, the spark in boyhood just goes dark.

Often, when people talk about freedom, they speak of having freedom from something. Freedom from hate. Freedom from slavery. Freedom from debt. Emma Goldman, on the other hand, talks about "the freedom to." Practicing freedom in this affirming way brings about re-alignment of one's approach to the world. We get better at taking responsibility. Seeing freedom as a 'to' and not a 'from' can show us how to help boys and girls to become.

Be careful with fire, Xavier. When curious, ask questions. When lost, seek help. Spirit grows from risks, but learn what wisdom means and how to let it in.

I warned the boy that fire was real. It can kill and destroy. Respect it!

I kept his matches and his kindling. I sent him back to class and called his father. "I want to let you know that your son is entering the fire years." He said thank you, as if we were brothers of the same tribe.

To this boy, no lies told, no souls crushed. Ahead, a chance to build a different kind of fire. More than that, my honest wish — for him walk a bright path toward a place different from those that circle around unending boyhoods.

Would that his fires be bright ones to lead us.

Locks

I am thinking about this little girl named Daniella who came to my school a couple of months into the year. Some thoughtful adult had taught her to begin each request with 'excuse me' followed by the ask. How she spoke got her, most often, just what she wanted — attention, a second muffin, a shoe tied.

Daniella liked to run away too. For reasons not shared with me, she didn't live with her mom for the first three years of her life. Then, child protective folks put mother and daughter back together. Daniella, about that time, started learning how to run. Fast! When I got a call this morning that she had run from the classroom, I knew I needed to pick up speed if I were to catch her. She could be anywhere.

That's when I stepped onto the yard and saw our gate, unlocked, wide open, swinging in a breeze coming over the bay.

You can buy locks, or parts for them everywhere. They sell keyed locks, digital locks, and huge locks that weigh ten pounds. An unlocked lock, however, is equal to an open door. And the chemicals released in one's body upon even the thought of a child that might have slipped away are among the more intense. Adrenaline, nausea, panic.

My own elementary school had no locks. How could that be true? An entire side of our playground had no fence. Is my memory correct on this point? What were we thinking back then? Now, I have a big sign on the door to the school announcing lock times and have cameras at each entrance to the school — the presumption: locked gates equal safe school.

As I increased my pace to 'search speed', my mind ran through a dozen renovation plans I had reviewed, each one sketching a different way to enter and exit the school. They all channeled people through monitored gates. All of them offered high fences with a lockable latch and suggested protocols to enhance safety. My school would become, once it is renovated, a modern-day fortress — ten foot fences made of black mesh and sturdy gates that slide closed with a muted click. Only the very few would have keys.

For today, I got lucky. For, you see, a gate that closes can also be left open.

When I saw the open gate this morning, how powerless I felt! If she had wanted to, she would find a way out. But today, Daniella did not get out. She hadn't even tried.

Instead she ran to my school's social worker for some in-the-moment intervention. Adults had not communicated, hence the sounding of the alarm and the ensuing search.

Safety is about assigning level-headed individuals to the appropriate places — and not sheltering behind the wall of what might happen. A good protector has to see and must refuse to blink. So far, I have not lost a child.

Noting my record, I pressed reset on my day. I walked beneath a smiling sun after all. Locks worked like tranquilizers, but they bought me nothing that could not be better done with a watchful and loving team.

Through it all, a girl like Daniella will find her way — because or in spite of our best efforts.

Queen

My school sits on top of a rock hill. On top of that rock, a playground. On top of the playground, a play structure. If you scramble up the ladder that ascends the play structure, you can stand tall over bay, boats, and the shipyards that extend for miles. So yesterday, the last day of school, I headed out the back gate to descend the hill and looked back up to take in the end-of-year moment.

That's when I noticed Akili.

She had climbed to the top of the structure and now had her eyes pointed east down a stretch of dry wheat grass that leaned toward the bay. I saw no one else on the playground. Grown-ups had all vacated so by five PM, only Akili, I, and a couple of drifters just down the hill remained. The crown of her head, because of where she had climbed, had now become the highest point on the hill.

Rail thin, unhinged, rag-tag, regal. I saw all of these things in a girl I had passed before without noticing. Though she had to have seen me standing nearby, no matter. She put in a pair of ear-buds and entered a time, realm and reason of her own. She pulled off her knit cap, and swung it over her head. At her back, the low, sinking sun back-lit her silhouette in smoky orange. Then she started to sing.

I can't wait to be queen!

No one saying do this

No one saying be there

No one saying stop that

No one saying see here

Free to run around all day

Free to do it all my way

Beyond the singing, her body moved with the pulse of drums. She danced with nothing but air to hold onto, wriggling her fifty pounds, flashed big teeth, pumped twilight air into her bony rib cage, and kept on even after her sweatpants slipped and she lost a shoe. She went at it with such abandon, I caught myself wondering — had she gone over to the other side? Did her mother know where this little girl was? Would she be OK?

I decided to let his song speak for the girl. I would take her at his word — that Akili could not wait to be queen.

I wish for many things. For example, that every girl at least once might know the expanse of arms outstretched, and the glee of full flight. Just once to stand on top, cloud kissing, singing out as if nobody cared and as everyone craved. Might I even wish such a moment for myself?

Half-way gone and still not yet. Not quite.

As I continued downhill, I laughed a bit. Up above, Akili kept singing. Drifters still waited and I joined them at the stop as the bus pulled up. Three of us stepped onto the bus together. When the door closed, I listened into the quiet. I studied my seat before I sat down and then took my place next to the scratch-tagged window. The ride home would take a half hour.

Oh to be ruler of this rocky hill, guarded by grass, open from all sides, singer of song, protected from nothing, obligated by no one, liberated from the second guess. In command of my words and free in my thoughts. At peace and at one with the full-on and resolute in whatever steps I choose.

Not yet. But, I know that my time — our time — is closer each day.

One

Among the first words a child learns is the word "no." "No" comes just before the word "mine" and when a child discovers its power, he begins to use that power to separate himself from others. Separation rituals show up on the playground, reinforced by painted lines, boundaries, zones, and cones. It shows up again in games where kids get divided into teams, some kids getting picked and others, not.

The opposite of separation — unity — also manages to shove its way in as well. Even when the moment feels unsafe, and even when a child feels most alone, kids can find a way to come together. The choice sits there, side by side with all the others. A kindergarten classroom helped me see how it works.

At 10 AM last Friday in Room 313, story time began. I sat in the back as Ms. Jacobs took a big book, lifted it up, gave it life, brought voice to the symbols, and poured a waiting world into children's open hearts and minds. Two five year olds, Daniel and Daniel, caught my eye, their chins upturned, mouths gaping a bit, eyes wide and ears receiving. I had broken up one of their fights just an hour before. But now, nothing stood between the golden thread of the message and their inner-most beings. It all got in — the words and the story beyond the words — into the core. Could these be the same two who kicked and cursed moments before?

Ms. Jacobs story telling — the way she spoke with such quiet urgency — guided a room full of five year-olds in coming together, sharing the spirit of a tall tale, and forgetting about the things that kept them apart. The type on the pages transmuted into light, color, sound, smell, and a message about the power of hope to defend against fear, the touch of grace that intervenes in the face of cruel slights — the abiding capacity to rise up and carry on even as we have lost most everything. Chaos from the outside became harmony on the inside.

Separation means us and them. Change the 'and' to 'versus' and you have hierarchy. From hierarchy comes oppression. Oppression leads to conflict. And conflict will lead to destruction.

I can't make in any plainer than that.

If a child looks at his options as got-mine-or-not, it's no wonder when things go south.

Daniel and Daniel had found a balance. Even today when they engaged in mini-might combat — whose ball, who's first, who is being mean — the finger-pointing and tears fall away. Union returns. It's part of the cycle.

After Ms. Jacobs finished her story, she told the boys and girls to go back to the rug and one of the Daniels tripped on his own shoelace, falling flat-out on the linoleum floor. The other Daniel stooped down, took his sometimes arch-enemy by the hand, lifted him up and asked "are you OK?" I was there! I saw it! No trick nor agenda. Just a good boy ready to step forward and help his friend.

Flashing your teeth and growling goes nowhere. Little guys still remember — at least at times — that the way forward is down a gentler path.

Offering

I stood in my school's upstairs window, tracking the shifts in a slow moving storm. Clouds dark and heavy had pummeled us that morning. Now came a slight pause. I estimated thirty minutes before another downpour. Enough time to get the kids outside for recess?

I thought so.

I hopped down the steps, made the 'outside recess' announcement over the PA, and listened as delighted screeches echoed through the halls. And, for the first several minutes, recess proceeded as hoped. Then, seven minutes in, a single, precise cloud let forth a forceful downpour. I blew my whistle and we all clamored indoors, wet, boisterous, clumsy, all accounted for.

But who was I kidding?

I turned back to scan the playground and saw one child, the quiet kid, Terrence Harrison, dead center on the basketball court, rocking side to side. "Terrence! Come on!" He didn't budge so I pulled my hood tight and headed back out. I discovered him coat-less, without shoes, clad in wet jeans and a soaked t-shirt.

"Terrence! What are you doing out here, man?" He made a clicking sound, but said nothing else. I reached out my hand. He did not reach back. Instead, he leaned forward, cupping something between both palms, holding it close to his chest. I couldn't tell what he concealed, but he seemed to be protecting it. Now what? In the rain I became impatient, declaring us both too wet for games. I hauled him up, and hustled us both toward the back door. Click, click.

When we stepped inside, at last the boy spoke — one word: "Look!"

He lifted his cupped hands close to my face and pulled back the hand on top. There, crumpled, vivid, but still dry, sat a bright explosion of geometry rendered from folded paper. Wa lah! A flower. He held out this fragile thing, beheld it with open-eyed wonder and then said to me, "Take it."

That brought the total number of spoken words to three, plus the clicks.

How this folded art survived I could not explain, And, likewise, Terrence persisted. I looked at the flower, at the boy, and then accepted, exhaling as I did so.

When we got to the office, my secretary scanned us both and asked whether she should call his mom. "No. Let's wait. But can you get him a pair of sweats and a blanket? He can dry off by the heater."

Such a small thing, this burst of color, cradled between his palms. He pulled up a plastic chair and took advantage of a warm room. I placed his flower on the heater grates next to him as he relaxed into to an apparent vigil. He was wet, calm, peaceful.

My impulse to scold passed. Instead, I observed him sort things out. I knew next to nothing about him other than the fact that he had presented an offering, simple and surprising. Perhaps I should have said thank you.

Thank you, because he slipped through the tightness that most days constituted my normal. Who had I become? As if my primary purpose were reduced to controlling out-of-order circumstances. Really? Please had I let that become my truth?

Divine nudges come all the time. Just when I lose faith in life, they return. They insist, and cry out. "Look over here! Listen to me." Message for today: Pay attention when a silent boy shares his secrets. He may offer something to a reluctant spirit, ever cupped between who he once was, and that which awaits.

95

We are a vulnerable species. Other creatures on this planet are far faster and far stronger than even the fastest and strongest human. I can imagine a roundtable of creatures – bears, lions, cheetahs, sharks, and so on chuckling when they hear humans speak of themselves in high-toned ways. And, when do we really get the fact that we're not all that powerful?

Victory

Showing up on time, everyday, has its rewards. Little Victoria, a third grader, found that out this week when she won the grand prize for perfect attendance — a triple scoop of ice cream on a sugar cone. To celebrate her victory, she chose vanilla!

This vanilla was said to be the best in town. For my part, I got to build the top-heavy cone and watch as her green eyes lit up. She paraded around and soon had a little string of sweet-treat friends who got to begging for one quick lick. Nothing doing, however. Little Victoria just kept moving and burying her round, red-cheeked face in ice cream. In about a minute, she wore as much as she ate.

In those moments, I saw this little girl in a different light: Tiny for a third grader, she wore her hair in a ponytail that came from the crown of her head and flopped around as she walked. Wearing her hair that way boosted her height a bit. Since she needed two hands to hold the cone, I noticed how tiny these hands were. Also — a tiny mouth, tiny feet, small ears. A small package of a child, now leading an impromptu parade with her edible attendance award.

With sun overhead and the asphalt kicking up heat, Victoria lost control of the cone when she went to throw her hair back. Ice cream — all that remained, became a star-shaped splat on her shiny black shoes. Now, the parade ended, her schoolmates giggled, and tears came.

She had no chance with this cone. I should have seen that. Even with a ballerina's poise and maximum focus. . .

Amidst the giggling, however, a fifth grader approached. The boy, Rafael, had won the award the prior month, and the heat had taken its toll on his award as well. In a few short seconds, the sweet-treat parade disbanded leaving only the tall (for a fifth grader) kindly boy, attending to the tears of the crushed little girl. What struck me was how the boy stuck with her, walked her to the bench, and even helped her by paper toweling her shoe so that it wasn't quite such a wipe out.

Wow, I heard myself saying. What a prince! I also heard myself wondering at the motivation and the gentleness of this boy. What was he up to? Why did he seem thus called to assist this girl? Were they related? I mentioned my questioning mind to my colleague, Jennifer. She looked at me — gave me a good look — and said, what if he's just being kind?

Well, what if? I had not considered that possibility. How might there be, not only this boy, but others, undercover among the rough and the tough, who carried gentle hearts within them, warm like the sun, but cloud-covered until the right moment? I thought back to my own days on the playground and could not recall having kindness (nor the courage to use it) to allow me to come out the way Rafael had.

My past is not my whole story. I can watch and learn. Teachers emerge at the right time. If I plant both feet on the ground and speak less often about what everyone else should do, I can continue to find the reluctant knight of my boyhood, that audacious open heart, who might today, ride on in.

Flying

Naptime in the Pre-K room. Short by one teacher so I am helping out. A pack of three, four, and five year olds do not want to sleep. They want to be read to, talked to, laughed with. Sleep is not on their list. But the teacher and I persist. Naptime is non-negotiable.

Five minutes later all but three kids are down and drifting toward eyes-closed innocence. I hear a couple of tiny snores. Marcus, one of three, becomes my project as the teacher takes on the other two.

Marcus squirms on his cot and peeks out from under his long dreads. I read to him but what he really wants to do is tell me he's five. He wants to slap a drum beat on his belly, and bounce on his cot. I convince him to close his eyes, telling him it's a game, and I say I'm going to tell him a story.

We have a little discussion about the world inside his head where he can open his "inside eyes" and see all kinds of things he can't see in the outside world. He says he knows all about that place. He tells me he wants to fly way up and then he covers his eyes. I ask him whether he can see the seagull flying to his left or the pelican flying to his right or the bay below where he might also see the reflection of his three-foot frame skimming the water's surface.

He shifts and gets still. I tell him to fly higher and tell me what he sees. It's at this point that he says he sees his daddy. He then tells me his daddy is dead but when he comes up here, the two of them can talk, see one another, and be friends.

I had not expected that nap time would take this kind of a turn and I find myself getting very quiet, letting him be and getting the sense that I am standing inside of a sacred place. I have been in the classroom no more than twenty minutes but I have a sense that I have stepped outside of time. I look across the room at fifteen napping kids, the teacher gives me a nod and I slip out the door and back onto the playground.

Later, still quiet on the inside, I am seated in a different room crowded with other principals. We are watching PowerPoint slides that cast a blue tint onto our upturned faces. The charts contain data about kids who are not making gains in academics and who seem to be stuck, falling further behind with each new school year.

The experts speaking to us have their points organized in clipped sentences, arranged in bulleted lists, set up to fit within ten agenda minutes. I am in my seat with my outside eyes wide open. Through the window, I see a grade-school child kicking a red ball against a concrete wall. The minute hand on the room's big clock skips a notch past the ten and moves that much closer to the twelve.

Just a day, just this day, just one little sacred day.

8.

April

Four by Four

"So, an ace beats a ten, right."
"Right."
"And you have three aces."
"Yep."
"And Enrique has three tens."
"That means I win."
"Again?"
"Again."
"Who's next?"
"Who's left?"
"Seems you are the last one standing."
"I'm good at winning."

Thief

Peter, a tall skinny kid in my fifth grade class had sunken eyes, a snaggle-tooth and hollowed-out cheeks. His arms flopped from his shoulders, unhinged. Kids called him the scarecrow, but not the one without a brain. He grasped opportunity and sought to outflank the wide-eyed among us. I sensed his edge and knew him to be meaner than the sum of his skinny parts.

He brought a new game to school one day — quarters. "Do you want to flip?" To play, you and one other player had to flip the coin at the same time. He would call heads or tails. If his coin matched what he called, he kept both. If they didn't, you went again. If they matched but were opposite of what he called, you kept the coins. That didn't happen much.

One Tuesday I noticed Peter's coin-stuffed back pocket. A line of boys faced off and went down. Flip after flip, Peter cleaned each boy out. I was last in line. Three times in a row we flipped, and in three, my pockets went empty. But, wide-eyed as I was, I knew something was off.

On Wednesday, I watched him work. He asked a lot of questions and popped out with his loud laugh. I plugged my ears and kept my eyes on his hand until I saw it — a fast flutter with the knuckle of his middle finger used to flip the coin just before he lifted his hand for the reveal.

The little thief! I didn't want to believe it. I called him out and cursed him out. You're stealing everybody's money!

To my outburst, he asked — "what did you expect?" With a big oh-well-too-bad he walked away, coins clinking. Since I'm holding this story decades later, I know that though he walked away, I am still here.

When something gets taken, something takes its place. For me, I held onto a promise not to get taken twice. What got taken away was an abiding sense that in this life, I could count on friends to take care of me. What's your game? What do you want? I'm onto you. Not today, thanks.

Any time you move on with hardness in your heart, even hardness well earned, it adds weight to the journey. And now, a pack of old stories, full of hard lessons and cynical proof points, want to talk to me again — to tell me that I need to give them another look. I see reconsideration of this kind as my own way of joining in this change called the Great Turning that writer and thinker Joanna Macy speaks of — mine being more of an inside job culling from the gritty playground of my boyhood.

This time around, a hand has to reach not for the familiar, but for the hand of someone unknown or someone I once hated. I ask myself how I would react if I were to reach back to find that it's Peter's hand in mine. Coming to grips with my Great Turning — that's how I can step up for myself in my own quiet way. Where we go now, we must go together. As above, so below. As within, so without. Thieves and saints alike. I can't see how we'll get there if we insist on going one by one.

Now

Each April, the hills around my school explode with dandelions. Yellow sunbursts pop open next to orange poppies and purple lupines. Tiny bursts of color bob among broken glass, scattered car parts, and non-native grasses. But it's the dandelions that send up those floating pom-poms of seeds— white and round — to drift everywhere in the afternoon winds.

On one of these wind-whipped afternoons, I met Alvie. I had seen this little guy before — a boy who could not speak, who kick-boxed with his own shadow, and who brought a fond grin to the staff member who supported him. So, when I say I met him that afternoon, I mean that I *saw* him as if for the first time as a floating pom pom came to rest on his up-turned nose.

He blew the white fuzzy shape up and followed its path as it settled on the bench next to him. Then he lay himself face-down on that bench and put the tip of his nose right up to the fuzz. He blew again and the pom pom wafted, settling a yard farther on. I heard him giggle — a free and high little laugh that spoke of delight. He scooted along the bench until he came nose to nose with the pom-pom again. Blow, scoot, go, repeat!

The particular benches that line the playground run along the chain link fence, interrupted only by the main gate and a couple of portable classrooms. That day, Alvie started on the east side of the yard in a counter-clockwise journey of the many benches, puff by puff. The waft, the giggle, and the soft return. I watched as he made the most out of next-to-nothing and I fell out of my worries, tumbling all the way back into this precise moment. That he could do that much meant this little guy worked magic!

When the bell rang, Alvie's helper crossed the yard to lift him up. She brought along his new-found dandelion friend and carried it indoors as she carried him upon her hip. I could see that she had discovered this little boy long before.

Unlike Alvie, I don't visit the here-and-now all that often. I experience 'now' as one more item on my check list of 'shoulds' as in you *should* spend more time in the present. Being in 'now' is a rarity that arrives when the spill over from yesterday and the tug of the yet-to-be lose track of me. In those moments, I can fall into that spacious little in-between.

Alvie inhabits this place with skill as he travels through it each day — an abundant realm of his own making, straight forward, free and safe. Though that's not a skill I possess, I have to learn to forgive myself for often flying through days without seeing this splendid banquet — and remember to take stock in a particular gift I do have - the ability to snag fleeting bits of this bounty as they waft by before my open eyes. Universes full, rich, and close as the tip of my up-turned nose.

To have lived and have missed this much would be like not living. Through Alvie, I am finding out how to take a second look.

Thin

James, a fourth grader, is a different kind of boy. Not because he is a mix of two races. Not for the bouncy clump of black and blond hair that sits like a wedge at the crown of his head. And at four feet, five inches tall, he stands at the middle of the pack.

But then you get to the paleness of his skin — skin with a hint of blue that reminds me of transparencies. He is thin, too. Maybe too thin. He has to cinch his baggy jeans at the hips with a wide brown belt. When a strong breeze hits him, it appears to ripple through.

And beyond these descriptors is something more — a capacity that I can point to but not prove. James is permeable. Everything, even a thought unspoken, gets in. He feels all of it. How would I name such a quality?

Enter "Big" (Leonard). A wide faced fifth grader with a solid wedge of bone beneath his eyebrows, he takes wide, almost lateral steps as he walks. He knocks into people and things as a matter of course. Still, I care about these boys as if they were my own, so yesterday, when their paths collided, I got engaged.

The sequence lasted no more than thirty seconds. James sat in a chair outside the office door. He had melted down in the classroom because, by his own report, his classmates had been thinking mean things about him. He said he felt safer near my door.

Then, Big approached. As he approached, he asked "What you lookin' at, freak?" and James lunged, scratching the larger boy on the neck. Big dropped to the floor and remained on his knees, in tears. I intervened just before a second scratch occurred.

"That boy just attacked Big for no reason." I heard one student comment after the blow-up. I might add to her sentence: "No reason that you and I could see." For James, the exchange amounted to reprisal. I didn't know that side of James, the boy just beyond the snapping point.

An intuitive boy like James makes me reassess my baseline. He won't get off the hook for his actions, but these circumstances are unique. I had believed that thoughts weighed less than words and words less than deeds. In a boy who can feel an intention as if it were a fist, lines blur. If I accept that James feels thoughts, words, and actions as palpable things, I question whether the world within one's head is a private one of little consequence. Does intent — either to harm or help — matter if it never rises to the level of action?

I watch public figures distance themselves from their own words and deeds. Truth might come closer if they lean in the opposite direction. I may have met a boy with capacity to feel silent messages and I want good to come of this kind of gift. James might, for example, show us how to lift others up. By thinking of sunshine, he might teach us how to bring light into the room.

Maybe people will never change. Should change come, however, it will first show up in children. As of yesterday, my hunch is that it may be here already.

Every memory, belief, experience, craving, pain or joy – the flow of all of these things adds to an ever growing river. It picks up speed and becomes harder to redirect. All things go in, nothing gets skipped and everything counts. In many ways we can find that we have been swept away.

Stuck

Stephanie, a kindergarten girl, began the first morning of her first day of school by standing still in the middle of the playground, telling me that she wanted to go home. She didn't cry or whimper. Instead, under her red knit cap, she repeated herself — that she wanted to go home and that she wanted her mom.

I walked up to her and made up things to say. Anything I could think of. Sure you can go home. Let's walk around the playground. Where did your cap come from? Sure you can go home. We'll go in just a bit. What did you get to eat for breakfast? Who's your new best friend?

Anything.

I wanted to get her around a corner and pulled into some other narrative. The sing song of her teacher's voice or even the prospect of a might-be-fun day ahead. Then, on her own, she stopped. One of her classmates caught her eye and she ran after this friend — last in line — as the class ascended the stairs. I will never know which thoughts allowed her to get herself unstuck.

Stephanie, just yesterday, reminded me of myself. I sat in my parked car. I kept the window rolled up and I searched for the strength to open the car door to go inside the building. Might-be's mixing in with must-do's in my mind.

I wanted to go home.

My day's start rolled in with a dream I had had the previous night. In this dream, I am driving on a freeway, following someone who then falls behind me. The car I follow drives down an off-ramp as I watch. I then speed forward on the freeway, on my own, without anyone ahead of me. This fact scares me. I get off the freeway at the next exit, I park, and I make my way on foot through alleys and crowded buildings, never reaching a clear endpoint.

How is that dream connected?

Later this same day at a meeting, I listened to five different principals recount factors that led to their successes — how they achieved astounding results in their schools. I thought about days in the classroom, listening to show-and-tell presentations from the teachers' favorite students.

But my question remained a humble one: how to acquire the courage to go forward on the days when I am stuck. Or when the memory of the previous day's body-blows still linger and the mind refuses to clear.

My long days arise not the facts on the ground. Endless mental rehearsal. Anxiety countered by daily confidence-building rituals, posting motivational notes, and seeking affirmation in the smallest things in order to reposition myself for what might be — or for what I might imagine.

Stephanie presents me with a puzzle.

What stiffened her spine so that she could move on? I am older, but not that different from her. I get pulled along by the might-be as much as I recoil from what I don't know. A flame just hot enough to light the next wick, encouraging words from an empathetic friend, curiosity that overrides doubt — or even the lack of a better idea. These things get me through.

Fibs

Fibs can be good things. They can shroud truths not ready for sunlight. They can buy time when the skin is still too thin. I considered these facts as I looked over incident notes I took today. A mean quick little sequence at lunch time led me to write the report out long-hand so that I could see all of the pieces.

My notes describe how a knot of students gathered near the basketball hoops. They recount the distance I had to scoot from the door of the lunch room toward the tightening ring. They tell how, even ten yards out, I could hear a familiar voice shouting "Get away from me!".

I had to push through the ring to reach Bishop Riley, a nine-year old. No secrets now. Someone had pantsed him and there he stood. His baggy jeans and drawers sat in a rumple at his ankles. He clenched his fists, cried, and swung at no precise target. One girl prodded him: "Pull your pants up, skinny little boy. Ooo my, look at those chicken legs." He tugged up his trousers and spat back: "I'm gonna break your little chicken neck. Brush your teeth you ugly little girl!"

"OK. Clear out!" I boomed. Children scattered. That left me to sort out the details with the still smoldering Bishop. "You wanna tell me what happened?" I asked. We both waited until his tears and rapid breathing eased. Other than naming Tatiana as the one who pantsed him, he said nothing.

When I come to places where secrets dwell, I recognize them as powerful places. Not places I enjoy, but the dynamics I do indeed respect. Scars from these places can last a lifetime. Rapid exposure of hidden things can call out monsters and ghosts that are, as Stephen King says, "Real. They live inside us, and sometimes, they win."

For example, even in the five seconds Bishop needed to retrieve his trousers, I chanced onto more secrets, like six welts that stood out on the back of his left leg or the fact that the girl who taunted him — and likely pantsed him — was his cousin. The two lived together in the same apartment, yet again a house of secrets in its own right.

I stood by Bishop for a good while to assess the damage. I then made required phone calls and dealt out consequences that seemed somehow insufficient. But for all that I discovered, instinct whispered that still more secrets remained beyond the shaming. A story before the story and one that was not my business.

Sun set. Sun rose and Bishop returned the next day. He stepped to the end of his line. He did not look at me and did not speak as he went inside. "Don't pry, Principal." I heard the voice of a former mentor, Eloise Brooks, advising me to "respect the dignity of privacy."

Truth has its place. Timing matters too. Bishop, like all little boys, is a storyteller. If he can learn to spin new stories, he might recapture that which was taken, and shape new truths so that they work in his favor. Tall tales buy time, and clear the way - a shot at a fresh start. A good thing for a nine year old boy and also for men like me.

Portal

Theodore, a red-haired nine year-old, cut across the playground before the start of school, stepping in front of me and tugging on my tie to pull me close for a whisper: "Did you see it?" "See what?" "The note that Jake and me put in your mailbox yesterday. Did you read it?"

Theodore blinked as I said no, I had not read the note. Even as I confessed as much to this particular red head, the other one popped out from inside the building to say: "He hasn't read it yet. It's still in his mailbox."

"Wait a minute, boys. Would you both mind backing up a little bit? Let me get in the door first and I will read it."

"OK. Don't forget" one said as they both dashed away.

Once in the office, I pulled a stack from my mailbox to find a smudged half sheet upon which sat a penciled sentence. I read it out loud: ***Meet me and Jake on the playground at 10:20 — before recess.*** My secretary stopped typing, and looked at me winking: "A mystery?"

So it seemed.

At 10:20, I stepped onto the lower yard. Fog touched down on the asphalt. Calm reigned. Perhaps the meeting might not occur? But then, two familiar voices pierced the peace.

"Principal, come on!"

"Guys, now tell me where we're going?"

"The auditorium! We found it!"

"You found what?"

They tugged me by the coat sleeve, talking as we walked, tag-teaming me with essential facts. Theodore had discovered the ***key*** first. He then told Jake and only

Jake. Now, I was third in line to receive access to ***the knowledge.***

They led me up the back steps to the stage. "Behind here." said Jake as he pulled back an old, maybe ancient, blue velvet curtain. There, I saw for the first time, an obsolete phone screwed to the wall. Half an inch of dusk sat like a hat atop this plastic artifact.

"Pick it up!" one boy barked. I did, but I handed it to Theodore who put it up to his ear.

"That thing's gross. Do you hear something?"

He said nothing, so I took the phone and placed it against my ear. I, too, heard nothing. I handed the phone to Jake, he listened into it for a moment, and then hung it up. They looked at me with truth in their eyes and asked, "What do we do now?"

No laughing matter. They ***knew*** the ways boys can that they had found a portal. It had become my job to advise them on how to get it to work. I had no desire to crush dreams. I thought fast and spoke:

"Gentlemen, if you have found real a portal here, they don't just stay on all the time. You have to find out when it works." Both heads nodded. "When you figure that out, we can come back. All of us will have to be ready. We need to get this right."

Juicy stuff hides in mysteries like these. I watched the boys walk back to the playground, leaning close to one another, whispering. Prospects and possibilities wove spells within them. I knew that kindred medicines like these can make a strong mix, carving openings like a wizard's knife. Only a matter of time before that same knife would cut through to dreaming's other side — a realm where sparkling keys dangle in midair. I counted myself lucky to be along for the ride this time through!

107

Shirley Chisholm said that service is the rent we pay for the privilege of living on this earth. It is the very purpose of life, and not something you do in your spare time. What about the act of being kind? Could this become more than an accidental by-product of good mood?

Tooth

A week ago, I bit into a day that had to do with teeth. By teeth, I mean the tooth itself as it grows in but also when it gets drilled or even yanked out. It began when little TJ approached me by the school gate, stood in my path, and held the right side of his face.

My tooth hurts, he whimpered. Open your mouth, I said. Then, under noon sun, on the lower right, I saw one tooth with a hole, ringed by black and brown. A huge cavity! "TJ, I can just about see through to your brain." I knew that tooth would have to get drilled or come out.

The bite continued. Kids came to the office with teeth falling out or getting chipped from chin-to-jaw collisions. Late in the afternoon, I heard one of my staff members comparing her colleague to a bad tooth. "Someone needs to yank that sucker out of here and throw her in the trash." Her co-worker fired back,"Then what?". An even crooked-er one will just grow back in her place."

By the end of the day, I could recite the tooth's life cycle up to its final rest on the steel tray in a dentist's office. I called another principal on the phone that evening and mentioned the message I had received from my encounters with teeth. She added: "Two years to pull it out and then you'll have to tear out part of the jaw just to make sure."

Ah yes. So much wisdom! From all, I pulled several little lessons that went something like this:

One bad tooth, chipped, rotted or otherwise out of whack, sucks the attention away from every other thing.

A good tooth — the one that sits side by side with the bad — goes ignored.

Pain from a bad tooth spreads quickly.

Whenever you tug hard on anything, everything around it gets torn.

Give a child an hour with a bad tooth and he will give anything to have it pulled.

But the comment from my co-worker comparing a person to a bad tooth that, even when yanked, would return more crooked than before, went to the root. Activist Julia "Butterfly" Hill, once asked "When you say you're going to throw something away — where's away? There is no away." Throw, yank, pluck, or pull. If you tell me — out of sight means out of mind — I might say sure, but just for a little while.

Painful stuff shifts around and changes places. The discomfort sticks around. Learning to contend with what is and inviting blessings that come from the quiet service of the good teeth — patient, humble, going unseen and under-appreciated, may open the way for a bad tooth to come out.

Bug

Eight children gathered near the tether-ball pole in a tight little ring. Arm over shoulder over arm, they shrieked, stopped, lunged, stumbled, but advanced. Approximate trajectory: due east. From my remote perch, I could guess their goal — to cross the yard. On the other side, a strip of grass awaited along with the chain link fence. I suspected mischief and approached.

The eight had their eyes set not on where they were headed, but on a point in the center of their circle — something I wasn't close enough to see. However, as I got close enough to hear, I could tell they had come to a decision point. Wait. Stop. No! No! Don't move. OK now! Go! Go! Go! Five other children — the rest of the ring — followed instructions as best they could.

Seeing me, Timmy, a third grade Samoan boy and ring leader, pulled back his braided black hair, put his index finger to his lips and gave me an order — Shhh! You'll scare the bug.

At that moment, I saw what they saw at center of their ring — a kind of grasshopper, big as a child's pinky. Yellow spots on black wings stood out, flapping over long green hopper legs. Then it jumped. Not more than a foot, but enough to make the ring jump along with it. Timmy whispered to me — "We're trying to save it." We need to help it get to the grass.

Meanwhile, Lawrence, a kindergarten boy in a red knit cap and bright yellow sneakers (not part of the ring of eight), approached the ring with a different idea. He, too, saw the bug and zipped around the ring wanting a better view. When the bug jumped and the ring stumbled, Lawrence shot through to the middle. I am the bug man, he shouted. He lifted his little foot and clog-heeled the yellow-dotted-hopping thing into bug meal in one efficient grind. Silence followed. Then shock. Crying. And almost a pummeling that I had to prevent with both hands!

What were you thinking Lawrence? A squished bug had unleashed plenty! We came to a full stop — undone by the agression of a small runt of a child — a little, speckle-skinned boy with a name like Lawrence.

Witnessing happens when you open your eyes to allow what you see to enter without filter. Stories, judgments and rationalizations flood in after, but the penetration of initial imprint can reach deep. It can highlight the distance between you and someone else or touch on how little you understand about how and why things happen as they do. Lawrence, I believe, delivered some form of opportunity.

In a bug's world there is no such thing as waste. Given the shortness of time and the urgency of circumstance, I take biting moments like these and ask what the bug's guts offered. Today, I got to share in shock. Tonight, I get to reach into that goo, at least in my mind, look at it, and let the juice stay on my skin for a moment. I get to forget about the particulars and sit with how it feels to feel what I feel. That may be how I learn from little guys like Lawrence, who out number me nine to one.

Push

It's 3 AM. I am sitting up in bed, wakened by a bit of unfinished business from the previous day that wants to roll up into a possible encounter in the coming morning. Thoughts and their associated impact are more direct at this hour so it's loud in this moment of solitude.

I breathe, lie back down, and start to slip under when a memory from two years ago pops in for a visit. I am watching a wiry kindergarten boy, Carlos, who is at the bottom of the slide struggling to push a second grade girl, Isabel, back up the slide. I also remember that she, among second grade classmates, is the heaviest. Her round, motionless body, angled head down in the trough of the slide will not budge. Carlos, with his strong little hands and new white sneakers, has met his match.

I can see the moment his body goes slack. He gives up, let's go, and pops off the slide. Isabel's eyes open wide. She lets out a high-pitched eek and plummets to the rubber mat below. Then, four first graders fly down after her, screeching as they flash by. The gaggle of children on the upper platform thins, and the play structure comes alive with motion.

What a curious episode to recall these many months later: Carlos surrendering, stopping, and getting out of the way. And here I am, reckoning with this particular memory and what this little messenger may want to show me. A question comes to the surface: what happens when I, as a leader, come to that place that Carlos has come to? I have launched plans, sustained an effort, intervened, pushed, and asked for help. Then a set of events and forces enters that tips the balance. What do I do when I slip past this tipping point?

To drop to one's knee and face doubts, witness reversals of fortune, and to surrender offer a chance to grow wiser and more open-hearted. After that shell has cracked, intuition, compassion, and vulnerability come forward. I call this shift acquiring the second sight.

When second sight comes, I have seen leaders develop the capacity to relax and become effective in different ways. As one principal told me years ago, after worrying to the point of harming his health, he had to let go and let events sometimes take their course. What he said is that he now has the freedom to sing whenever and wherever he wants to.

If I could pick and choose on a path toward perfection, where would the discovery come from? It was never a choice to cherry pick the traits and events I'd prefer. Celebrate all of it! That must be the message.

4 AM now. I will be up for work in an hour. But this unrequested reverie wants to let me go. Counting backward from one hundred, I pull the covers up under my chin, look at the streetlight outside, and hope to catch one more hour of communion with my friends on the other side.

Up

Yard duty Monday morning began with clouds punching across a square patch of blue above our playground. Then, in the span of half a recess, a storm front arrived in full and paused overhead.

Temperatures dropped and I turtled up in my big coat, preparing for the wait-and-watch. If a storm broke, I would rush the children inside. If not, we would tough it out together. Outdoor air, even if cold, did wonders for little brains.

I keyed in on one lone six-year old, Kylee, who sat on the tire swing, dolled up in red mittens, long stocking cap, and a powder blue coat that swallowed her whole. She had her eyes on the sky and the swing to herself. Meanwhile, two dozen other first-graders huddled in their puffy grays near the school's double doors. A few boys blew 'smoke' rings with hot breath. No child spoke more than a word here or there.

Just too cold!

Then my ears popped. Barometric pressure had to be dropping still. Chills and an ache in my knee told me my wait-and-watch would end soon. I slid blue hands from coat pockets to ready my frozen whistle. Time to give the signal, thought I. That's when Kylee rose up on the swing, looked toward the clouds and uttered a single word.

Snow.

On cue, snow fell, soundless and ample, white and vanishing on blacktop. I tucked my frozen whistle in my coat pocket, looked up to see what was happening to the children:

Half a dozen boys popped their heads from puffy hoods, looked upward, and repeated Kylee's chant. Snow. The word rose up in rising steam from the mouths of wide-eyed first graders as they drifted into the center of the yard. Then Kylee opened her mouth, stuck out her tongue and waited. On that pink flesh, flakes lit for less than an instant.

Both to the left and the right children clustered on every corner of the playground. All stood with faces toward the heavens, surrendering to the prospect of a flake landing on the tip of their tongue. When the bell rang, not a single child moved.

Present moment. . .

I hear people talk all the time about becoming more present — and how we can find our way back there when we get lost. Presence exists in the instance before a storm and in the wait for the snowflake that falls to an outstretched tongue. Like a lot of things that matter, now exists everywhere and nowhere at all. If you try to see it, capture it or reach for it, you can make it disappear.

I saw kids scoop up snowflakes that melted in their mittens. They chased them and licked them from tree limbs along the west edge of the yard. I saw a single flake alight and melt on the tip of Kylee's warm tongue. Then I saw two dozen six year-olds stand silent as snowfall stopped and clouds opened to cold blue once again.

In truth, we don't ever get to the here and now by grasping. We know it from trace memories or from anticipation. A mystery that may come just as a storm arrives, and may linger on in the moments after it goes. Children can point out where to look. What happens next is up to us.

9.

May

Sunshine from the West Side

"What ya doin'?"
"Watching the birds fly."
"You mean the seagulls?"
"No, look up there."
"Wow! A hawk!"
"Two of 'em."
"Ms. Garcia says those birds are a sign."
"A sign of what?"
"She just said if you see a hawk, pay attention."
"What do you think the birds want you to know?"
"I can't tell yet."
"Just wait. Something will come."

Knots

Six kindergarten girls sat in six little chairs that lined the breezeway outside the cafeteria. I had told them to plant their little backsides there in those chairs and remain until otherwise directed. Sit they did, arms folded, pouting lips puffed out, polished dress shoes dangling and kicking. They were mad for life.

Kindergarten graduation would start in forty minutes.

Kimberly spoke first, tight braids sticking to her tear-wet face. And why are you mad? Angela pushed me! I did not! (Now it was Angela's turn). You made me fall out of my chair! You're a liar! I did not! And so on. . .This apparent misunderstanding arose out of a scuffle during the final practice run through that morning. Jessica, the most talkative of the six, told the story this way:

Wanda forgot where she was supposed to go and sat in Antoinique's chair. Kimberly forgot which chair she was supposed to sit in and then she sat in Angela's chair. Well that's the wrong chair. Mrs. De'Angelo told her that! Then Angela got mad and pushed Kimberly and she fell on the three other little girls. It's all Wanda's fault.

According to RuPaul, your state of mind eventually shows up on your face. His advice, therefore, is to think beautiful thoughts. I did not see evidence of a beautiful thought in this bunch. Their faces got stuck in I'm-mad knots, a true contrast to their fluffy dresses and primped and adorable heads.

Graduation would begin in less than thirty minutes.

I had managed to get them parked in these chairs, but now they were refusing to move. Stubborn little bodies ready to stick it out for the long haul, full to the brim with the need to be right.

One abiding experience I've had with unsolvable problems — they don't exist. A problem is something that exists in a person's mind. Since minds make problems up, a problem is as solid as thought itself — gone when the mind that owns a particular thought changes or ceases to exist. Six kindergarten girls committed to perpetual hate — anyone could see that their stubborn pride would lose energy and cease to exist.

However, I had less than twenty minutes.

Family members had started to arrive. They scanned my six little damsels who still had their arms folded, each one a fortress ready to resist change for all time. Then Antoinique slipped off the chair and went to the restroom. Wanda decided to follow her. Two more hopped from their seats when Auntie Clair came up the walkway with congratulation balloons.

We were down to two — plus me. So, I went inside.

The last two standing (or sitting in this case) lost their audience. I peeked out from inside the auditorium, now filling with all kinds of people. Angela looked at Kimberly and Kimberly looked back.

They grinned and ran to the room back stage where their classmates had already lined up. So ended another battle. So vanished another cause — as important and permanent as all that had gone before — and all that might come after.

On one edge of the Big Empty — I find a cliff. Beginning and end float just beyond that cliff. Energy flows in silence and also pure freedom. A week ago, I stood there on my little cliff, looking out and feeling into this empty place. I got that it gave birth to everything.

Kiss

Evelyn kissed Hector. That much appears to be true. Little else about this fifth grade lip lock came to light except that they kissed near the dumpster, held hands for about five minutes and sat together on the monkey bars. I never saw the kissing but I did see them afterward: he in his low-slung creased Ben Davis pants and white T-shirt, she in her muffin-top jeans and lace top.

What I did see? Two kids squirming, a shy giggle and Hector, the 10 year old brave bull, posturing. I chose to give these children a bit of space. Chalk it up to Spring, but I knew what might come next — a discovery that a tender moment can end even as it begins.

Then, surprise, Evelyn kissed Luther. The count rose to two kisses in one week!

Easy-girl gossip exploded as little groups of fourth and fifth graders — not to mention third graders on the inside track — clustered north, east, and south to break the facts down and mish-mash on the closest thing they had to scandal.

Luther, boy number two, had big lips, big eyes, and a soft voice. He passed for a fifth grade version of the total package. Reports indicated that as Hector turned his back and stayed on the basketball court, Luther and Evelyn hung out for kiss-day two — again on the far bench by the dumpster.

Then all of that commotion ended too.

No one said that impermanence is painless. Efficient and relentless — yes. I have the Zen circle painted on the wall of my office and next to me at home. The circle comes from a much older image of a snake eating its own tail, creating and destroying itself in an ongoing cycle.

With Evelyn, I get to see where things begin, what a random moment might someday mean and where a small step today migh want to lead us. Long roads start from such small steps.

But if I could speak to Evelyn so that she could hear me — I would talk to her young soul — the one just now learning to awaken. I would tell her — I see no fodder for teasing here. Instead, on the day of the first kiss, the one with Hector, I did see Evelyn as she took the boy by the hand. She looked to see who was watching her. What did people think? What did she think?

Momentum can be awesome. Even small things on a playground exist as part of a larger tumble that can carry us for years until it drops us in dust. Running away combines with chasing after. I chase, desperate to grab what I can't reach, aware that if I look back, I'll see fangs closing in to swallow me whole one more time.

That's how cycles progress from one day to the next — as inescapable steps toward an ending and a beginning. We don't escape the wheel, but instead learn to revolve with grace. Then, if only in our stories, we spin tales of playful lives where we make our own rules — where our little souls get loose for a moment and seize the opportunity to fly free.

117

Religion

I had a smooth know-it-all fourth grader in my school named Leland. Leland Washington Carter III to be exact. He was a talker and knew that fast talk could help him slip out of many a tight spot. He had a sparkling charm that won him unusual latitude among his peers and teachers. He knew that language had power and he could spin a story with deft speed. His charms made him stand out. He was a favorite, but also one to watch.

Then, a change came, turning young Leland from a fast talker into a wide-eyed and quiet little man. His new-found silent ways intensified over a period of two weeks. When I pried, I never got more than a few intriguing bits shared in private from his three aunts — that he had been with his family at a weekly church service, and that in the context of the service one Saturday, Leland became silent and — to use the words his aunts used — received a "visit from the prophet."

Amen, amen.

When week three came, I had little more than an uneasy feeling to go on. None of his family responded to calls. I made a call to social services to ask for guidance. That same day, Leland stopped coming to school. Through the neighborhood network I learned that the Carters had moved. No one had a forwarding address. I was left with unanswered questions and a deep wondering about what might befall him in his next home.

I struggle with an uncomfortable relationship with what I don't know. I can fill in blanks by inventing little happy-ending stories, but I am awe-struck with how little I know about the lives of the children I serve. Ignorance is part of living. At three pounds, an average adult brain has 100 billion neurons, 100,000 miles of capillaries, and one quadrillion connections. But with all of this capacity, the best I can hope for is an "A" for Effort. I will likely never know where the truth exists in this case and can learn only from my reaction to what I didn't know.

Total understanding of another human being is a kind of perfect geometry. A sphere. I can want to keep a child safe, but I can fill in the blanks with stuff that I make up. So ironic that schools place the index finger of hush on the lips of truth. To etch out solutions in the midst of the unknown and the inexplicable leaves us working with unlikely outcomes. I don't know Leland's story, but I know that working on his behalf blinded by my own bias leaves me with an incomplete shape and not the perfection I'd seek.

Simple facts speak their own blunt story. They may bring tears and it may make us frightened. Shutting it out makes us no stronger. Learning comes from opening wide to a totality of knowing — and through the spine to see the come-what-may. May the inexplicable become the known, may the boy somehow thrive, and may I use this loss to build greater skill using what I can't explain to inform what I can.

Jerk

Two weeks back, I had to pull all balls off the yard during morning recess. The cause: a high stakes form of one-fly-up that began with blasting heavy red balls high overhead, and then watching them descend like bombs. Luck held for weeks, but then, a little kindergartner, Melvin got bonked and went down. Game over.

I wanted kids to get exercise, however. So I sought the perfect replacement. Then it came! The sponge ball! I bought twelve of them in playschool colors. Even a direct hit in the kisser from one of these, I thought, could not harm anything but a boy's pride.

Morning of the first day, I tossed these balls out to a pack of eager fourth graders. They snagged them from mid air the way a hound pulls down a tossed stick and ran to the far side of the playground. Then, as if pre-coded for battle, they faced off in two lines. Assault and reprisal began.

I watched. Bell rang. Injury count, zero. Not bad, I thought, as I gathered the red, blue, and yellow into my bag.

But remember this: whenever you get together people — even the meekest — a jerk will somehow get into the mix. No soft lighting or modern furniture can banish this truth. So, on the third day, a new variable entered: we had a bit of rain. Not much, but enough to leave puddles. And what sponge ball doesn't like a puddle.

A blonde boy named Max — Maximus Harcourt Witherby III in full — red-faced rumbler with a bad temper and round behind, discovered that by dunking these balls, you had a whole different game. Water bombs flew fast and hit hard. As I chatted with moms, casualties increased. Then I heard Maximus' cackle. His laugh was always bad news.

I turned in time to see Henry, a thin Asian boy, black hair precision parted down the left side, setting his sights on Max. Henry hurled a slobbering sponge orb with conviction and purpose. Splat! Of course! A direct hit accompanied by a muddy wet spot eight inches across. Max, now out, should have stepped aside. A rule is a rule.

You're out, Henry said. Max refused to yield. I approached and told Max to stand down. No he said — this time to me.

That's it, I barked. Turn in the balls. We all play the same game or we won't play at all. Game over. Line up.

As I shoved the balls back into the little net bag, I wondered whether I had handled the situation in a beneficial way or whether the jerk in a boy triggered the jerk in a man.

This evening I am reviewing the rules — real ones and not the ones in the book. I don't yet understand why the algorithm works as it does. I do know that it takes one. One hero to turn the tide. One leader to take it over the top. One jerk to take it down. Max, on this third day, got to be that jerk.

Open questions as I look toward tomorrow: how do you advance your goals, even with a jerk in the mix? Or when leaders sit it out? How can you move on, even on days when all the heroes have decided to stay in bed? Good questions, I think. I am ready for answers from any source.

We fall all the time. Some falls are quite spectacular. News can later surface in the harshest possible light. And still, folks move to the next. In that after-shadow, healing begins. No band-aids, icepacks, or pats on the head matter. Mostly it's nothing more than time.

Lunch

Time for lunch. As always, I walk among cafeteria tables and peer down at what kids have to eat. What they bring and how they lay it out says a lot about who and how they are. For example, red-headed and freckle-face first grader, Derrick, has pulled out a peanut butter, jelly, and wheat bread sandwich smashed like guts in a Ziploc bag. The "Ziploc" has held, but not by much.

Then, across from Derrick, sits Anna, with her bangs precision cut and with both shoes tied. She lays out seven identical plastic containers. She has opened the first one — a little blue tub topped off with blueberries — and has lined up six more peach-colored tubs behind this one. "I will eat what's in 'em one at a time!" she declares as she tips the tub to let a tumble of berries roll to the back or her throat.

I see two little angels in sparkling shoes who console one another as one looks down upon her fallen strawberry, now mushed on the floor beneath her seat. A few feet away, two scrappy boys toss diced carrots into one another's mouths. Throughout the room, children toss back carton upon carton of chocolate milk - sweet elixir and a top tier trade item every day.

Lastly, Jon, who barks and laughs from beneath a clump of curly brown hair — occupies a perch at the end of the table. He snags good lunch prizes from the boys on either side of him. And more! When the unassuming Jasmine (across from him) turns her head, he plucks a wedge of an orange from her wide-open lunchbox. Within seconds, he has assembled a lunch that tops most others in the room. I intervene to return the goods to their rightful owners and my lunch lady slips him a milk and a piece of fruit.

Problem solved, I posit.

Then, a burst of wind muscles open the two big doors that lead to the yard. Leaves spill across the floor and a flutter of giggles flies up. Kids declare that the wind is the same that howled the night before, taking down power lines and tree limbs. It's back, they holler. It's back!

In the commotion, I look back to Jon who has set aside the humble grits provided. Instead, he has collected a new pile of prizes. He has a real eye for quality. Note to self! Not one of his classmates' protests. Lunch slips from their minds in the crescendo of conversation.

In all, nothing goes wrong. Just a few minor adjustments. Otherwise, the room pops with the spirits of children.

Yesterday morning, a friend read Hafiz's Tree House poem to me — perfect words to mark out this moment: that I am conducting the affairs of my lunchroom universe, presiding over a rambunctious party as if from a tree house that dangles on a limb in my heart.

Between pockets of down draft comes delight. Pure, wonderful, and often unnoticed. Why not let joy expand unchecked? Why not, sometimes, let children be just as they are? Tomorrow will rise and will bring what it may. Today, I'll order my lunch all you can eat.

Dust

Princess makes things up. Not that she lies. Instead, the dust she stirs blows from some hidden place and forms into shapes solid enough to collect into stories and give her a beginning and middle that might tumble toward an end.

With her shiny black hair tied back neat and tight, this ten year old girl came to school today dressed in the same blue sweatshirt she wore yesterday. As she arrived, however, I got a call from a panicked woman, a nurse who worked at our nearby clinic.

In short sentences, she described a girl she had just seen being choked outside a coffee shop. Forty year-old guy in a brown tweed jacket — the choker. She told me she had stepped out front and in between to intervene. But the girl and the man walked off. So she, seeking resolution, called every nearby school.

Do you know this girl?

I sat at my desk listening to the description — black hair, dark blue sweatshirt, neat, maybe ten years old. There, framed in the door to my office, she stood. Princess. No, could it be? I asked the ten year old to step through my door. Red marks on her neck. A tear in her collar.

Ma'am, I will call you back.

Facts blew out as short puffs with periods. Brown tweed belonged to uncle. Parents had left her. Mom lived somewhere in Mississippi. Never called anymore. Tweed throttled her since she was four. He choked her today because she had eaten candy without asking. He choked her last week for forgetting her homework. A month ago for talking back. Whatever.

Her gathering windstorm began when she was five. Pinning, throttling, smacking, and the backhand slap. All included. She could not remember the number of times. You have the right to safety and no one has the right to treat you these ways, I said. And she, at age ten, had such old eyes.

"Stop asking," she said "Just let me be. I am standing here, not there. Don't ask me about what happened. Let me be."

Each morning, I sweep the playground. Clearing away the day before helps me start over. I work my way around the edges, "pan-picking" a hodgepodge collection of dust covered discards. Another principal told me that you can't sweep yesterday away. Still, I keep sweeping. He even suggested that I make friends with the dust. It might be all you've got, he said. Make peace with it.

Redemption is an active force — a movement that calls for give and take — thrust and yield. Princess tells me that she wants to forget so that she can change. On this tough day, it's as simple and impossible as that.

Cleave

I like the idea that my thoughts are private — that a thought might become known only when I write it down or say it out loud. A "private thought" implies that I can think a thing but do not have to act upon it. I can pretend I am not accountable for it. Thoughts, I think, do not count the way actions and words do.

Last week, when an autistic girl refused to get on the little yellow bus at the end of the school day, I got to re-assess the "private thought" theory. I got called over the loud speaker to help in a bus situation. When I stepped onto this bus, I found the girl, the driver and the girl's teacher, teeth clenched, spitting out curt phrases at one another. The girl, Martha, wouldn't sit down, wouldn't shut up, and wouldn't wear the mandatory harness. Both the teacher and the driver leaned into this girl and even I could "hear" them cursing in their heads.

Then, Martha and I made eye contact. In that instant, what popped into my mind was how she and I knew each other. She had called my name during her talent show performance earlier that day. "You rock, Principal John."

So, in the moment our eyes connected, I smiled and called out her name: Martha! It was spontaneous. Then she sat. She stuck her hands up so that I could slip on the harness that she had to wear. It took ten seconds.

What made Martha change? Could it be that the girl *felt* the driver and the teacher sticking her with their thoughts?

What, then, did she feel when we made eye contact? So much for the privacy of thought.

An idea, even unspoken, exists. Real, sharp, biting — or gentle and loving. We lack ways to measure this truth, but there it is. Even if I refuse to admit what I'm thinking, it still shows up.

How far does this truth go? For example, when I write an incident report about a child, or when I think harsh things behind the closed doors of my office — when I speak unmeasured things to a confidante miles away, is there something that slips out and touches the target of my musings?.

In my grade school, all of the boys feared one teacher and went great lengths to avoid her. She spoke as if she were sinking and I can recall being puzzled at how such kind sounding words managed to come out of her mouth when I felt she was sticking me in the ribs. I can still picture her twisted smile. All of that stuff in her head got out, no doubt.

So we really can't hide? Maybe not.

As within, so without. To pretend that I am not on full display is missing the point. What I do want to become is a pioneer of openness — to live as though everything — thoughts included — mattered and I might stand up and be counted for all of it.

Done

I have a hard time with endings. I get wrapped up in my causes and then I don't want to let go. I have surrounded myself with people who hate to quit as well. We reinforce one another by sticking around when the many well-intended others have left the building. We speak in soft voices of what tenacity has given us — insights, wisdom, lives saved.

Then, there are the other folks — those who seem not to flinch as they walk away. They laugh at non-quitters, and caution us not to drown in our own holy water. Mission-driven people on one side and the hard hearted pragmatist on the other. The back-and-forth perpetuates itself.

How can I work in a way to stay healthy and balanced? Is there an honorable way to take a pause and step to the side?

Last Friday was the last day of school. I stood in the hallway of the second floor, listening into the growing silence. That little voice in my head piped in — "That's that." I felt some tightness in my joints and neck. I had thought to stay late and wrap a few things up, but instead, I knew it was time to slip out. I was done. As I stepped out the front door, I got a picture of myself driving down the hill, with the school shrinking into a stack of painted concrete rectangles in my rear-view mirror.

But then I noticed a bit of unfinished business following me in the form of a second grade boy. Jashawn had been my office companion for the final month of school. In the last week, he had run out of places to go and had burned bridges with all but a couple teachers on the faculty. His daily rages damaged property and injured kids. One-to-one supervision, parent-teacher meetings (when mom was sober), rule bending, home visits, treats and incentives — none of these topical interventions could change the fact that he left his apartment each morning to escape chaos and addicted adults, only to arrive at school filled with people who knew Jashawn for the harm he caused.

Even by second grade, he had said and done things that could not be forgotten. As an institution, we were done. But now, he was walking by my side, asking me whether he could come back to school on Monday, though it would be a school without his classmates. Then, he smiled at me, reached into his top pocket, and put on a pair of reading glasses as he beamed up at me. The glasses were mine, snagged from my desk or so it seems.

Journeys, when they involve people, may end when we say so — or may not. They don't end just because they're unhealthful or because they don't yield change. They also don't end just because we walk away or close doors. If there is inevitability to an ending, I have yet to know what signs would indicate as much. As I go into work next week, I know there will be a child tapping at my window, smiling, saying hello, ready to begin again.

Playground

Two kids, second graders, jockeyed for position the in morning line up, just after the second bell rang. I saw these two boys starting to go at one another, but I was about thirty yards away talking to a parent. Thirty yards seemed like a big distance to close as the taller boy cut his thin shoulder into the littler guy's torso. The little guy had these big lips that began to quiver. As I pulled up, he was trying to stand tall to make his stand. He started shoving back, demanding his spot.

They were two little men with their creased jeans, skinny arms, and rooster chests, sticking accusing fingers at the other, getting into it about one another's mother, who got there first and who would kick whose ass. I separated the boys, listened to their stuff for about three seconds, watched the hot air steam around their heads, and then did what I always do by putting the little guy first, and tall-n-slim second. Case closed.

But the case was not closed. Cases don't close quite so fast on the playground. I turned as if to leave, but then spun around just to check- and no surprise to me that I found the larger boy with his face up in the smaller boy's face. Tall-n-slim wanted to brand the little guy in a permanent way.

That's the way we burn it in when we are young. Who has the power and who has something to prove? What stuck with me on this day wasn't so much about the boys roughing it up, but about how much it reminded me of two dads challenging each other the night before at a board meeting, getting in one another's faces, still very much the little men they had been years ago on some playground somewhere. Everything to prove. I have just as many stories among adults that play out same as they do on the playground.

I know that child still lives in me. When an angry parent gets in my face or when I get nudged out in the supermarket line, it all lights up. My options reduce to a kind of stark either-or metric. A Zen priest mentioned yesterday during a sitting that years of meditation can add in a bit of space — re-introduce a split second of choice — to let air back in when it gets smoky. That tells me how, when kids spend time claiming turf, blaming others, and fending off threats, the mark that gets burned in on the playground returns as that part of the psyche that needs to breathe fire in order to feel alive.

What do I witness every day on the playground? If the element is fire then the asphalt is an anvil and events there are the blacksmith's hammer. I call all of this forward into my present experience as a leader and ask of myself what I hope for others, that I can hear through the smoke and see through the bright orange to the place past the first reactions where silence reigns and water flows.

Paunch

Today, at lunch duty, I stood between two long lunch tables. On both sides sat several dozen five year olds. My task, opening milk cartons. Child hands carton up, I take carton, do the slow peel back of the spout. Then, I return carton to the closest hand. Next?

As I opened the sixteenth or seventeenth carton, I became aware of a little pat pat pat on my belly. Milk cartons kept coming, so I ignored it and pressed on, but the pat pat persisted. OK, so what's up? I looked down to see Juan's small hand patting my belly in a small circle.

"Juan, what are you doing?" His saucer-big eyes connected with mine.

"Principal, how come your belly so big?"

My response: "Eat your lunch Juan."

He took my advice and went back to the rice and chicken dish — the featured item on the day's school lunch menu. But the exchange gave me pause. I took an instant to notice this little guy. I saw him every day, but now I saw him as if for the first full time. He had spiky hair and wore a blue and grey striped T-shirt. He had all of his teeth and a huge grin. Next to him on the lunch bench, two scuffed brown boots. He also made the most of the lunch table with parts of his lunch spread out a foot and a half to each side of him.

To myself I remarked — what a happy boy.

Then I saw an imprint where he had patted. And, for sure, from my vantage point, I indeed saw a paunch. Juan, meanwhile had already moved on, head down in his plastic plate or turned away to chat up his pint-sized friends. I became another 'whatever' in the five year old's mind.

He spoke in short burst of immediacy and electricity. Zap to the left, then a quick laugh, and then three more bites jammed into his still-talking mouth. I stayed stuck a few frames back on the part about my belly. I got something of a quick rush where my life flashed and I remembered, once again, that I am temporary.

Oh, that's right. . .

Coming alive involves learning to see. Seeing my body change and avoiding the temptation to look the other way — that's the opening Juan gave me. His summative statement came as a blunt truth, like calling out the color red or the state of the four-square ball — flat! No judgment. Just a declarative comment. No point for me in getting hooked on wishes or memories. Describe, capture, celebrate, and move on.

When I get nudged — or patted — my awareness kicks up a notch. I hear better and see more. I make way for little voices to cut through the din. I pause and let a given moment sink in. From there I can gain access to something just a bit bigger than I might have predicted. I might be wise to pat my own paunch and say thank you.

To you, Juan, I bow.

10.

June

Bringing it Home

"When's your last day?"
"Tomorrow."
"Wow! That came on fast."
"I know."
"Are you ready?"
"We been ready. We are all packed up."
"Do you all know your new school."
"My mama didn't tell me everything."
"What did she say?"
"That it's time to move on."
"Good luck."
"Thanks."

Revival

Raymond, stout little boy with a loud mouth, popped off first: "Dead rat in the trash can! Dead rat in the trash can!" The scream caught my ear. And even from across the playground, I could hear and see him pointing into the dented can. He kept up the racket:

Dead rat! Eeuuwwah!

Six seconds later, two children ran to him. Then three more. Then nine and soon a knot of little bodies closed in a ring around Exhibit A. Screams bounced off screams. The crowd grew beyond thirty, and now the situation required a direct response.

Crossing our playground from corner to corner, even at a brisk pace, can take a minute. Much can happen in sixty seconds. Here, even as I crossed, a string of pint-sized town criers approached to provide me with a shifting report. First, the story of a dead rat. Then, an account of a dead bird. Last the rumor of a cat. "Dead" remained a constant. All else was in flux.

Three girls dashed into the building to bring out Mr. Anthony, our custodian. He made a slow approach toward the crowd, and brought along a short-handled shovel and broom. We arrived at the scene together and leaned in for a look.

There, beneath a stack of potato chip bags and boxed juice containers, I saw a big, pink tail, too big for a rat but motionless for sure. "Looks dead to me," I think I said. "You got this?" I said to Anthony. "I got this, Principal."

He jabbed the shovel through debris as children sucked in air and held their breath. When he got underneath the critter, he could then pull it up. A wet matted body rose up, and new screams went out. There, flat out on his shovel, lay what looked to·be the biggest dead wet rat we had ever seen.

See, blurted Raymond. A dead rat!

That ain't no rat, Anthony said. It's a 'possum! No such thing as a rat that big.

He lay his dusting cloth over the little animal, paused, and with shovel extended front-ward, made one slow 180 degree turn. Then, we marched in a slow-jazz processional, all fifty of us, onward to the dumpsters on the other side.

Stay back, boys and girls. Anthony shouted. Step back.

When we reached the dumpster's edge, Anthony lifted the little body, and paused again. But here we should have known we were not finished. Not at all. In fact, in the midst of Anthony's pause, one more surprising thing happened. The opossum, thought to be dead, sprang up, locked eyes with the crowd, and jumped from its shovely funeral bed. The screech that rose up this time — as principal and children dove for cover — may have been unprecedented.

When we lifted our heads, our matted, wet friend had fled.

It came and went like that. Discovery, death, and revival. Anthony, sudden minister, now stood silent. But his grade-school congregation began storytelling and bean spilling across the yard. 'Possum' became monster, able to jump twenty feet, a creature that could fly and become invisible. For me the moment stood on its own terms. Anthony's first words following the silence: We don't die till we do.

Gratitude for the critter that can play dead. Awe for a creature that can rise up. The miracle of a death-bed revival. Such are the wonders and mysteries I'll carry home today, more alive for having witnessed it all.

129

Invisible

I once knew a girl who was almost invisible. Her name was Jasmine and she was a second grader. I do not mean that she could not be seen. Instead, I mean that she had found a way to avoid detection.

One day, I watched her descend the stairs with her classmates and walk out onto the playground. She flinched as she looked out on the asphalt. Balls flew and kids screamed. All of that noise, noise, noise! Please just make it go away! For an instant, I looked away from her to speak to a teacher and when I looked back, she was gone.

Not so fast, I said to myself. I stepped away from my conversation, and took a short walk to find her tucked around a corner, in the shade, out of sight. She was singing a little song to herself. I let her be but made a mental note to locate her each day to learn more about who and how she was.

On this particular day, she re-emerged from her corner when the bell rang, joining her class in line. She trembled a bit, remained silent, standing stiff and tall, looking up the stairs as her teacher came down.

So, why get nosey about a child who wants not to be seen? My curiosity arises from a hunch that break-through insights may lay tucked away within nearly invisible children like Jasmine.

The challenge is about how to draw out someone intent on disappearing. Straight-on approaches fail, as even by second grade these silent types will have created a dozen places to hide within themselves. Jasmine proved to be an emerging expert at avoiding an uninvited inquisitor.

Meanwhile, I continued to get barraged by noise-makers like "D". His name is Dominic, but everyone called him by his nickname. For a second grader, he was the picture of smooth. High-fives, low-fives and plenty of "hey, what's up?" to the third and fourth graders. As Jasmine practiced disappearing, D strolled across the black-top. High-speed kick balls missed him. Four-square players paused to allow him to pass. He was a playground king and impossible to avoid.

Someday, I may find a way to prove that an elementary school playground is the starting point for everything that will later appear on the global stage. A microcosm for the future of interpersonal dynamics and a canary-in-the-coal-mine for approaching changes that will pummel the planet and the human race.

If even a fraction of the much anticipated changes do come to pass, all of us will need a complete re-alignment of our operating assumptions. Could answers be showing up now on the blacktop? Might they be coming from the very children we have ignored.

I can't think of a single good reason to waste anyone. Since I know a great deal about what the high-pitched playground "confidence kids" have to offer, I am eager to turn my investigation elsewhere. The prospect that millions of hidden gifts may find their way into the sunshine helps me keep some space inside for what might be. All I need to do is to stand still and keep quiet.

Skin

A call came in by my direct line that Ms. Erikson's new second grade student, Benjamin, had run from the room. Last words as he ran through the door: I want my mom!

Benjamin's teacher was a big woman and her chasing days were over. On warm days, her feet swelled. She made a flat confession over the phone: " You get the big bucks. You chase him. I will never catch him. I've got a class to teach."

I grabbed my walkie-talkie and headed out the door. This curly headed, big eyed boy didn't hide well. I found him in less than a minute at the far north side of the playground, sitting criss-cross on the corner of a four-square court. He had his back toward the school building. I approached from the side and called his name. "Benjamin, what's going on?" He didn't move. I stepped closer and that's when he blew up.

His explosion came in screams — Get away from me! And in hates — I hate this school! And in wants — I want to go home! Two neighbors walked by and looked on. Here we were, working it through on a wide-open playground under a full morning sun.

My message to the front office: Hold the calls. I may be out here a while.

I stepped ten paces away and sat on the edge of the last bench next to the yard's back gate. His screams continued. I determined it best not to carry him inside. My apparent options: wait and watch.

As I sat, I tried to monitor what was happening with Benjamin. I noticed the flush and the fade of his skin as his emotions rose and receded. As I watched his color change, I started asking myself questions: Who is this little guy, anyway? What's happening just beneath that flush?

I also noticed things about myself. His outburst reminded me of a time in grade school when a bigger boy stole a red ball from me. I remember how he taunted me by holding it over my head. Come on! Get it! Grab it! Like Benjamin, I blew up and flew at the older boy, swinging, slapping and screaming. The bigger kid backed up and I can remember his face. I'm sure that I shocked him.

Skin hides a myriad of things. I have to adjust and redirect these energies underneath even as they conspire to show up in actions or comments that I can't take back. As much happens under the skin now as when I was a boy. I get plenty of practice, however. So now, on most days, I can keep my cool. Benjamin had no such sophisticated system.

The vulnerability of a thin skin is something all of us share. Old-school coaching tells us to tighten the jaw, and strut through the stumbles. But my skin, like every man's, is nothing more than a membrane. I feel it all and all of it shows up somewhere, somehow. As I sat waiting for Benjamin to calm down, I wondered who ever thought we could get stronger by trying to be tough.

Benjamin. No one gets an easy ride. Today, I am here for you so that you can be there for someone else tomorrow. Whenever you're ready to talk, I am ready. Waiting, you'll soon discover, is a big part of how we teach and then, how we learn.

I am standing on the playground behind my school. I am looking at the housing projects across the street. My head is full of a flurry. I am on edge. I walk and talk to myself. " Why am I doing this work?" Then, a red kickball slams into the fence just a few feet from my face. I snap to. Wake up! Notice! The red ball of truth. Let me in! You can see much more with your eyes open!

Roof

When I entered the office last Friday, I knew right away that the central heating system had gotten stuck and wouldn't shut down. I started opening windows. Outside, a storm had started to move in. Inside, hot air closed in, cooking up a reheated version of yesterday's news.

Even wall clocks drooped so that an hour on the wall melted into five on the floor. And there, in little chairs outside my office door, four first grade boys sat, sweating, waiting for my judgment — the same four who sat in these four chairs yesterday. I felt nothing close to gratitude as I began counting the minutes. Time: 10:00AM.

Would we make it until 11?

I peeled off my elbow-patched coat, loosened my tie and looked one more time at the clock. 10:04AM. I knew I needed to get up, get out, and take a walk. As four pairs of first-grade eyes watched, I stepped into the hall and headed for the roof.

My school has three floors, but also an additional bird's nest of a room on the fourth floor. Climb three flights of stairs, go through the little door marked 'roof access', and ascend one more flight. From there, crawl out through a hatch that leads onto tar-and-gravel. On top, everything unfolds — landmarks in the four directions, light from above, and an entire city below.

I stepped out and extended my arms to each side. How divine to take in the cool and the damp. A chill came through my shirt sleeves. Colder than I thought. Above were the clouds, huge, waiting for a silent signal to rumble in. These thunderheads towered hundreds of feet up. I could see a pair of gulls circling among them. I fell into quick reverie — a question I asked as a boy:

What makes clouds fly?

As a boy, I could watch them for hours. They had many powers — could go wherever they want to. No limit to pathways in the wide open sky and nothing there to get in their way. When caught against mountains, they could shape-shift and move on.

I wondered whether clouds could talk. I read records of vanquished cultures — peoples who could speak, one person to another, without making a sound. Records of such exchanges — heart-to-heart and not mouth-to-ear — point to something beyond the spoken word that opened onto bigger and bigger skies. Communication of this kind sidestepped the limits of language. People, if these records are factual, talked to one another just as if they were clouds.

My reverie drifted to Bell Hooks, a thinker and activist, who writes that what we can't imagine can't come into being. For me, it was the cloud story again. If I see myself as a two-bit scrunch behind a piled-high desk, breathing yesterday's re-heated exhales, and fanning a reproving finger at fidgety first grade boys — what kind of sky is that? I stood on the roof and watched for a moment more as silent clouds passed.

Big medicine in clouds assured that even the most doubtful among them never falls. Ten minutes of cloud bonding and the first drops of a downpour brought me back. Just this much was enough to free me from the side effects of stale air. I fixed my tie, and pulled open the hatch and prepared for re-entry. Thank you, thank you, I heard myself whispering thank you.

I stepped in through the hatch to try the day one more time.

133

Fire

David, a five year old, walked through the back gate of the school. He held up six fingers to show the number of superpowers he had that day. He held up a different number each day. No matter. He just wanted me to know he had back up should he need that extra boost. Then he elbowed his way into the mix around the play structure and the day began.

This need for an extra boost — and the practice of announcing a number as he passed by each morning — began after the second day of school. On that second day, he looked up and said "I'm going home." Then he cinched up his jeans and pulled his knit cap low, and took two steps toward the gate. He stopped, got quiet, and sat on the bench looking at his shoes until the bell rang.

On the third day, superpowers arrived.

Months passed with no further incident. Then, a week ago, he hit another bump. A classmate called him a girl and this shot got in. David has straight black hair to the middle of his back and he knows it makes him different. By the time he came to me, he looked ticked. He again said "I'm going home." Nothing more.

I already knew that David was turning into a little leader. His burning imagination had captured six or seven kindergarten boys who followed him to all parts of the playground. In his games he led them through swamps, into volcanoes, and on hunts to capture the blue alligator. In every game, he could flatten every enemy without exception. But now, with his head hanging and his spirit snuffed, he was the tableau of sad.

Dan Mulhern, author of **Everyday Leadership**, often incites people to lead with their best selves. He says a leader's fundamental purpose in serving people is "to protect their life and love their spirits." I believe these words to the core and used them to guide my next steps with David:

I made up a story about Fire Man. Fire Man, I told him, could take you by the hands, spin you around and lights you up. Heat and light would work through every dark spot, chasing out the darkness. Fire Man appeared whenever you needed him, but you had to ask.

Not one to stand on ceremony, the boy held up both hands, grinning. He promoted me to Fire Man status so I took both his hands and gave him five spins, telling him to make some noise. No problem! After he gave out one piercing howl, I brought him down. He looked up, cured, and said thanks. He then took off toward the play structure, chased by three of his classmates. End of story.

While the boy said thanks to me, I got the gift — an extra bit of fire that helped me see that I am as small as I decide, or as free as I choose. To lead with my best self, I have to burn out the worst. Fear and doubt take space that belongs to a much bigger, more adaptable leader. I got to witness magic working for David. I now know what fire can do — and not only for a five year old.

Slap

Of all the options in the gallery of minor slights — pinching, biting, kicking, scratching, punching, hair yanking, and slapping — the slap stands out. The slap, as it turns out, may have a purer heart than its cranky sisters in this rogue bunch.

I came to this conclusion last Friday after fifth grader Elena Fuller cranked her left arm back to deliver a roundhouse slap to the right side of Dwayne Thompson's laughing face. Not a golden moment by any means, but the efficiency of the exchange made an impression: Dwayne stopped laughing and even stopped speaking. Whatever the perceived injustice, the crisp crack of this slap on his soft cheek brought sudden silence to a once rambunctious mouth.

I told Elena to turn around, take five steps — and no looking back. Dwayne got the same instructions. They stood back to back for four minutes. I then took them to a quieter spot. While the three of us sat there in our little in-between, I called Earl, a kindly, former principal and a mentor to me. To my surprise, he answered. I told him the story and also shared how a big part of me wanted to give Elena a high five.

Ah. Happy Friday. Principals never have anyone to talk to, do we? Do you really want to talk about this? Yes Earl. I called you if you'll remember. Please, help me fill in some blanks.

Look, Earl said. You have a little girl in front of you right now who slapped this boy because she didn't know what else to do. Ask yourself why she slapped him. What's her story? When did she get her first slap? At some point, she learned to get the message across this way and I bet her story begins with a hand print across her own chops. The boy, for his part, is just as helpless. They can't go back, so you've got to help both these kids move forward.

I said to Earl — I don't want these kids to get the wrong message — that smacking one another is OK.

Earl cut me off — Some people prefer to bunch things together. These folks will tell you that hitting is always hitting. Wrong is always wrong. Everything comes in one color or the other. Don't waste your time they'll tell you, thinking about this stuff. . . But I am telling you that thinking is never a waste of time.

First of all, actions and choices come one by one, not in stacks, piles, or bunches. I don't believe that your little girl should have hit anyone — but when I used to dive into these situations, I always needed more to work with than 'either' and 'or'.

Second, remember that a slap happens with an open hand. Slaps wake you up. They get your attention. Punching, kicking, biting on the other hand — all of these are meant to hurt. That's their sole purpose. If you want to hurt someone, you choose something other than slapping. I'll let you take it from here.

Gee, thanks Earl. . .

I took the kids to my office, knowing that next steps had to include the usual reprimands and consequences, but I wanted something more than the same stale bread. I decided to wait the way my father used to, hands stuffed in his empty pockets, eyes angled skyward. He could wait a long time — all day if need be — for a little voice to drop down and whisper a hint or two about what comes next.

That day ended and it is now Sunday. Plenty of time for the angels to sing before school starts tomorrow.

Alive

On an apple-crisp Tuesday morning, one of my second grade teachers invited me to join her students in their start up activity. They lined up shoulder-to-shoulder on the playground and I took a spot on the farthest end. She then told us to close our eyes and get as quiet as we could.

Listen, she said. Sniff twice. Feel the cool air.

She described what she called an inside ear and asked us to listen with this ear as well. What could we hear? A couple of kids giggled, but the teacher reminded us that this inside ear worked better when our eyes and mouths were closed. I followed instructions.

Then, counting down from ten to zero she told us to open our eyelids slowly, as if they were heavy doors. She suggested that we should see everything that the sun touched as if for the first time. Then she closed by saying that the real gift was hers because she got to see treasures in our bright and upturned faces. Good morning! What a fresh start!

In those second graders, I saw wonder and surprise. Those emotions stood in contrast to my focus — at least at first — that had drifted to a broken slide, and a tardy staff member slipping in the side door. I didn't miss the point of the activity all together, but I noticed how my eyes opened onto a different world.

Most days, I skip this sort of start-up step. When I open my eyes, it's still dark out. The day hits with its random force. I stumble around a bit and run a mental list of incoming events and situations. Often, the list I create has little to inspire, but these kinds of days, I explain to myself, are inevitable part of what I do. Time to lean in and be thankful for employment.

Flashing back to a big meeting I attended in Sacramento years ago, I recall lots of middle management folks packed the room to take notes on the latest mandates, rules, and guidelines for one silly thing or another. I am a long way from remembering any specifics of that meeting. But, I can still picture one older woman who stood up and introduced herself as a former assistant superintendent. When she spoke, I noted her hardened face, bent back and reddened eyes. It was the hardness in her voice that made me most uneasy. Would that be me? Is that what happens to old leaders?

Might waking up, by its very nature, push us toward a better relationship with the what-if? For me to harden into a tight and battered site leader, wouldn't I have had to ignore or deny a great deal? Plentiful evidence confirms the following: each day brings an unknown. Even if I try to shut out the mysteries and the wonders, they still happen — I just end up the loser for having missed them.

Maybe it's better to allow the experience of being alive squeeze me. Let it stink and smell sweet all at once. Or let me ride it as if I were riding a twisting road with my eyes closed. What I want after all is for a way to see the whole of what is — even if once in a while — when I once again open my eyes.

Deep

Everything needs to change. Or so I hear myself say to myself. When I walk the halls for my school, drive down 24th Street, or even when I look at how my shirt and tie don't quite click, I am making changes — at least in my mind.

The ambitious scope of these change-wishes extends to just about everything that exists. That bulletin board has the same displays as a month ago. Check. Maybe I could raise funds to get these fluorescent lights ripped out of here. Check. Who ever thought that pink tile was a good idea for a hallway? Check. That house across the open space there. . .Why can't they just flatten it. Check.

Then, I read and hear from sundry sages that nothing is permanent. If you don't like your internal weather, wait an hour. It will change. Everything changes, I'm told. Change is the only constant, they say. Hmmm. Then how is it that the stuff that wasn't quite right yesterday — and last week or last month — remains unchanged today and will likely stand as is tomorrow?

Might this statement be more accurate? Everything changes though not as one might hope. Or, I change, but everything else stays the same. Or maybe, we can relegate change to the realm of mystery. Here is my take away: each day's mindless antics (even where the actors change) look much as they did the day before. Systems that didn't work continue not to work. Cycles big and small proceed as they did centuries ago.

Take fourth grader, Leo, for example. My school has the perfect banister for fourth grade boys to slide down. Leo discovered this fact. Baggy jeans wrapped his thin frame creating the right physics for a fast slide. Of course, I had already put in the change order; a perpetual restriction from using this stairway. That order went in when Leo was in second grade, and in third. Even after one incident where he lost it and flew headlong into those pink tile walls, he continued his pranks.

If I managed to redirect Leo, but then, the following week, another boy, Eduardo maybe, picked up the same behavior, would that amount to a change? When antics just shift from one protagonist to another what might that imply? Oh great sages, where are you when we need you?

Change may be often topical. Erosion, peeling paint, a fading flag that flaps each day atop the pole. But adjustments within people. .deep stuff. . where might that level of change reside? Reactive behavior, blaming, and refusal to take responsibility — that which gets us caught — I can report first hand that these tendencies remain till the last.

Here's one more prospect: Every challenge we face in our homes, schools, cities and beyond, points to how deep we would have to reach if we were to hope to shift course for anything other than an evolutionary collision. Is this built-in obtuseness a sort of pre-loaded cosmic "STOP" button — that forces us to do, think, or say things other than we might normally?

If kids are any indication, then people must be among the most stubborn of all creatures inhabiting this planet. Liberation from ourselves may have to come right between our eyes. We'll either figure out how to wake up, bruised but grateful for another go, or we will balk and slide off that big banister in the sky. Of course, I'm hoping that after the fall comes the rise.

Is that the way it has always been?

You can't pretend to fit when you don't. Forcing it sets you back more than knowing when to quit. Patience can buy you time till the way becomes clear. A natural fit exists, that perfect sweet spot where the whole thing comes makes sense. Don't bother to fake it. There is a right fit for everyone.

Window

When it comes time to go, you get messages from everywhere. A thought turns to a nudge, and then to a shove. Tasks that you completed with ease become challenging. The mind refuses to generate convincing excuses for further delay. A great voice whispers, then rumbles, from deep inside your cells — Hit the road!

Today, for example, I stood in the doorway to my office. Light came in through an open window at the west end of the building's main hall. I stopped for a moment — just to listen to my insides. Are you sure? I heard myself say . .

I felt something bump my heels. A push broom! My custodian, his hat brim angled down, had swept around the corner and into me. He was moving fast and trying to bust out his shift in short order. I turned, looked at his broom, then at him.

"Hey! You trying to sweep me out the door?"

"Oh sorry boss. I didn't see you there."

"Go on! Goodbye!"

Then Camilla, a compact girl with short black hair, sprang up the stairs from the deck below, darted in front of me, and hopped toward her classroom — the one across the hall from my office. She stopped in the doorway, shoved her hands in her jeans pockets, and turned her blue cap backward. What's not right here? She looked at a pile of debris at her feet and became quiet.

My kaleidoscope, she said. It's trashed!

A red and blue paper tube sat crunched and tucked in among the other bits and shreds of student work, all torn and dusty. She looked up, and burst out with one loud "Oh well!"

Her giggle bounced through the halls. "Bye bye!" Then, she kicked her heels, bounced along the shiny floor toward the light at the far end. She opened the door, stood for a second, and then slam. The door closed and the hallway dropped into silence.

I looked into my office. Last time. When I closed the door, wind sucked it shut like a vault. I dangled, then released my keys into the drop box by the office door. And then I turned westward toward the light.

Try skipping! the voice told me. Get out! Go!

Sweat, hugs, stings and bites will find ways to come along wherever I go — star-crossed kisses shaped by how I choose to kiss them back. I might think of even the hardest times as bits of stardust left along roads where I had walked — roads I left for higher ground.

I can hold to this day's brooding cross-road as an invitation — a genuflection telling me to bow my head and admit the presence of something powerful, even if bittersweet. I can accept a moment like this as a lesson in how, on a planet as small as this one, you can never run away. You will, in time, end up where you began.

My heart pounded at a steady pace. I walked toward nowhere in particular. I wanted to stop long enough to find the way-inside boy that never quits — who can crawl out from under the weight of the done-and-gone. Door opened, sun hit my upturned face, and last day melted into first. One more good old, never-before chance to be alive!

Gone

All but one of the roads that lead away from my school lead downhill. I didn't get this fact's importance until I stepped onto the playground one morning and saw ten boys, lined up along the chain link fence, looking out, hands gripping the fence. Stepping up next to boy number ten, I asked what was going on.

Look down the hill. There it goes! Can you get it?

A big, brand new, red bouncy ball was leaving us — a top-quality kickball — and like every ball before this one, it cleared the fence and escaped. I saw it begin to roll and I knew I would not be able to get it. I got to watch it pick up speed, pop on a bit of street debris, and land moving faster than before. There I stood, powerless, just like the other ten boys.

Each time a ball goes over the fence, we get to practice how to give things up. I am a witness to daily launches of kick balls, soccer balls, and every other round thing. I have become more accustomed to the loss, having stood there at the fence, watching a ball fly over my head, smack in the center of the street, and then move on.

At times it may linger there as if deciding which way to go or whether it will go at all. But, in the end, gravity compels the journey downward, making the ball pick up speed, and then comes the vanishing. On a rare day, a kind driver will hop out of his vehicle and snatch one for us, or a ball might get caught on the tire of a parked car. More often, they go for good.

We don't get to hang on to things as long as we want. They stay in our lives as long as they do. Nothing except

practice blunts the punch of a loss. Just about everything we treasure goes — even our very selves. As the loss unfolds, time can seem to slow. I can imagine that I am hearing the little voices of wise spirits whisper unto me that which I have always needed to know about how to hold and honor that which I cannot own.

Tonight I got to visit with those wise little voices again. During the day, we had hosted a big festival on the playground. Music, children, snow cones and a half-dozen balls booted over the fence never to return. Our school sometimes measures the best days by the biggest losses. That's one way to do it.

I closed up the yard gate after one last child walked out. I went in to lock up the building. I was the only one there. Standing alone in the halls of an empty school building serves as a kind of proof that the building itself is alive. Dark corridors, silent but full. Lights out and just the wind tunneling down hallways and under doors.

Creaks coming from behind the building's old and weathered skin. Does it make sense to say that empty schools are full nonetheless — full of a particular kind of empty?

What I get to witness in a moment like this one is the arrival of an ending, advancing with jaws open, eating everything that had been in order to make space for what needs to come next.

That's what the long-gone kickball would have wanted me to know.

Afterword

I began writing these stories six years ago. The final collection contains one hundred blacktop parables, but eighty others had to sacrifice themselves at the side of the road for me to reach this hilltop. Each story brought me closer to my heart and my purpose.

When I began writing, I found myself in a time full of doubt and fear. Dreams kept me up and work made me anxious. I didn't find the source of these fears but I decided to work through that time by writing – recording my journey — so that all that I had experience would not vanish with me.

Over these years, I shared these posts with anyone who would read them. I thought I was writing about leadership at first, but my stories did not look like the writing of researchers or academics.

Now, in looking back, I know that I was re-crafting my own narrative. I know that story telling is a human right. These collected stories cover the nine months of a school year from mid-September through mid-June. They offer the truth of what I have witnessed.

I wrote these tales for my own awakening. I also wrote them for the child in you. May they bring light to us all in a time where the need for light has never been greater.

For those of us who lead from the middle, our best hope at turning things around is to speak our truths so that the unfolding that ends in adulthood remains visible, viable, and vibrant no matter how long we live.

Made in the USA
San Bernardino, CA
15 November 2015